MARGOT ASQUITH

THE GLASS OF FASHION

SOME SOCIAL REFLECTIONS

BY

A GENTLEMAN WITH A DUSTER

AUTHOR OF "THE MIRRORS OF DOWNING STREET"

> The cymbals crash,
>   And the dancers walk;
> With long silk stockings,
>   And arms of chalk,
> Butterfly skirts,
>   And white breasts bare;
> And shadows of dead men
>   Watching 'em there.
>   —*Alfred Noyes.*

> "You ask me if I am going to 'The Masquerade'?
> I am at it: Circumspice."—*Cornelius O'Dowd.*

ILLUSTRATED

G. P. PUTNAM'S SONS
NEW YORK AND LONDON
The Knickerbocker Press
1921

18757

PREFACE TO THE AMERICAN EDITION

In a letter to Mary Gladstone, the painter Burne-Jones, who was also an idealist, broke into lamentation over the quarrels and trivial animosities which too often exist between men of genius.

> My dear [he exclaimed], if twelve of these men would hold together for one ten years the whole aspect of the world would be changed—and twelve men did once hold together and the whole face of the world *was* changed.

What might not happen to this world, let us ask ourselves, if the two great Commonwealths, which have inherited, with the language of Shakespeare and Wyclif, the moral idealism of Milton and Lincoln, held together for a generation—not for any political end, however worthy, nor to impose their military power upon mankind, even in the cause of universal disarmament, but merely to define, make manifest, and exalt the moral values of human life?

Because I believe such a unity is possible, nay, is in the nature of things, I, heartily wishful for the moral comradeship of America and earnestly seeking the

intellectual alliance of America, venture in true friendliness and with all due respect to address this personal
word to the American reader of my book, *The Glass of
Fashion*.

I would say to him: Since the questions with which
this pamphlet deals are questions of importance to your
country as well as to mine, do not, I pray you, let its
English setting stand in the way of your American
attention. For the same contagion of materialism which
is attempting to destroy us is also attempting to destroy
you, and the same depression of a false science which is
weighing down the human spirit in these British Islands
is also weighing down the human spirit in your United
States of America.

You, too, have your Repingtons and Margots; and
you, too, have the same heroic but ineffectual goodness
which here in England vainly seeks to stem the mon-
strous flood of modern animalism. We are both of us
cursed by the same inheritance from the last century,
the inheritance of a scientific falsehood—that "nightmare of waste and death," as Samuel Butler called it,
which is "as baseless as it is repulsive." We are both
held by the same philosophical paralysis which has
crept over the human mind ever since the dark and disfiguring shadow of Darwinism fell upon the fields of life.
In both of us the cancer of cynicism (that arrest of the
moral tissues, that check in spiritual development)
preys upon the divine faculties of our humanity whereby

alone we can respond to the joy, wonder, and beauty of existence. With you, as with us, life has lost its way, and neither for you nor for us can there be hope of coming into our true inheritance until we have recovered those title-deeds to immortality which our fathers threw away when they set out to wander in the wilderness of this false materialism.

If, then, there is hope of a Renaissance in England, there must also be hope of a Renaissance in America. And the same spirit which can give this new birth to England can also give a new birth to America. Therefore let us take counsel together, and if we come to a like decision in this great matter, let us set out as one spirit to change the face of the world.

Now this is my conviction: Out of the stagnant fen of materialism into which humanity seems at this time to be fast sinking, with all the glories of its mechanical achievements and all the splendours of its earliest poetic enthusiasms, like a sun that has had its day, we can be lifted only by one of those great waves of moral enlightenment which in the first century of our dispensation saved mankind from the darkness of paganism and in the sixteenth century rescued Europe from the clutches of an iron dogmatism.

If we would live we must overthrow the false science which is destroying us, as the fathers of Christianity overthrew paganism, and the fathers of the Renaissance overthrew authority. In both of those great epochs of the past, humanity escaped from the prison-house of a tyranny into the open country of freedom. Life, feeling itself at the point of death, flung itself far forward into an untrodden future. With us it must be the same. We cannot niggle with the oppression which is destroying us; we must throw it off, throw it far from us, and go forward to a new dawn in human history.

To this end I suggest that we should look at Fashion, which shows us the set of the human tide more strikingly than any other manifestation of contemporary thought. I suggest that we should take Fashion seriously. I suggest that we should take the measure of the leaders of mankind, those who set the fashion of daily life, whose influence is the moral climate in which we breathe and form our opinions. I argue that if their measure does not square with the highest hopes of the human race, and does not square with the deepest needs of the human spirit, then we must put those leaders away from us, and find others more worthy of man's place in the universe. This can be done only by right-thinking, but right-thinking which is militant.

With you, as with us, the fashion of daily life is set by those who have sacrificed to a false science, almost without thought, the one great secret of joy, namely, *faith in a creative purpose, faith in man's immortality.* It is that secret we must recover for mankind, and we can recover it only by making remorseless war on this false science. It is useless to make war on luxury, or to make war on folly, or to make war on the odious ugliness of materialism. We must make war on the thought which brings such spiritual malformations into existence. Right thinking, armed with the sword of truth, must destroy wrong-thinking drunk with the dope of Circean lies.

Our first reason for making war on that false thought is this: it is destroying us; our second reason, that it is not true.

Darwinism not only justifies the sensualist at the trough and Fashion at her glass; it justifies Prussianism at the cannon, and Bolshevism at the prison-door. If Darwinism be true, if Mind is to be driven out of the universe and accident accepted as a sufficient cause for all the majesty and glory of physical nature, then there is no crime of violence, however abominable in its circumstances and, however cruel in its execution which cannot be justified by success, and no triviality, no absurdity of Fashion, which deserves a censure: more— there is no act of disinterested love and tenderness, no deed of self-sacrifice and mercy, no aspiration after beauty and excellence, for which a single reason can be adduced in logic.

On these grounds alone Darwinism is condemned; but it is condemned also on scientific grounds. Darwinism explains only the least interesting changes and modifications in physical structure: it does not explain the movement of life or its manifest direction towards excellence; and as to origins, and as to the final destination of all this vast and orderly movement of life, it is dumb. Nevertheless this false science, this utterly inadequate theory, which was challenged at the outset, doubted by great men throughout its victorious course of dominion, and which is now acknowledged by every thinker to be but a partial explanation of a few not very important phenomena, still rules the mind of the multitude. The mob believes in Darwinian evolution, believes that the universe is an accident, life is an accident, and beauty is an accident. It has made up its mind on hearsay, and incorporated into its moods, without realisation of the logical consequences, a theory of existence which is as false as it is destructive. And this mob, composed of all classes, carries the destinies of the human race. It is not with the philosopher and man of science we have got to reckon, but with a doped, embittered, and now incurious mass—the laggard and joyless bulk of mankind which is blundering because it walks in its sleep.

We are in the hands of cynicism. All those high and beautiful things which the noblest sons of men have cherished in all generations now stand at the peril of brutality; and no statesmanship can save them. The one insurance against calamity is a new "climate of opinion," universal as the air we breathe. The mob must be awakened. The windows of the house of life must be flung wide open. The mind of humanity must live.

It is for those of us who hold that without faith in the immortality of man there can be no right thinking to assert that great faith with a crusading valour, to assert it and re-assert it, until humanity recovers its spiritual dignity and the long labours of evolution find at last their final impulse in the conscious co-operation of mankind.

INTRODUCTION

With no disrespect to the House of Lords, I consider there is no position higher than that of an English country gentleman.—PEMBERTON MILNES.

THE grave moralist concerns himself with evils so flagrant that no one is in any doubt as to their nature. He is the policeman of society, keeping his eye on the burglar, the publican, and the prostitute. The satirist and the comic artist, on the other hand, are concerned with such matters as fashion and manners, matters which seem beneath the notice of the grave moralist, but which nevertheless exercise a more potent influence on society than the teaching of philosophers, the programmes of political reformers, and the machinations of the criminal classes.

Folly, not vice, is the enemy. Our curse is not original sin but aboriginal stupidity. It is human to err, inhuman to practise iniquity. We blunder rather than sin. Few men set out to reach hell, but most of us are for ever losing our way to heaven.

Folly, as an aberration, is laughable; as a fashion, as a rule of life, it is disastrous.

The object of this book is to convince people of two

truths hitherto obscured by tolerance and careless thinking—the danger of Folly: the value to a liberal State of a valid Aristocracy. I would persuade men that Folly, which has never cared a snap of its fingers for the satirist, is a pervasive poison which corrupts the entire body of a people, and that a democratic State, if it would make a powerful contribution to the higher life of the human race, needs at its head a small body of enlightened people conscious of its duty to the Commonwealth and religiously determined to set the highest possible standard in manners and morals.

To those who say that satire is the proper weapon to be directed against Folly, and declare the suggestion absurd that the artillery of moral indignation should be levied against such trivial things as the excesses of Fashion, I would make this simple answer: Satire is the instrument of the cynic, not of the critic, the tool of the destroyer, not of the builder, and its victories in history have been chiefly defeats of virtue, not destructions of vice. Folly survives. And it survives in the cool assurance that the satires which have been directed against it are so many bouquets laid at its triumphant feet.

The reason of this, I think, is plain enough. The satirist is a spectator. He makes amusing or stinging remarks on the spectacle of human activity, rather to obtain the applause of brother cynics than to assist humanity in its work. He is, in some particulars, a great danger to the State, for he tends to make a community believe that what so frivolous or ironic a spirit considers laughable cannot conceivably be worth the attention of serious people.

The critic, on the other hand, is a worker. He seeks to help the labour of humanity by sound advice and true guidance. His utterances are not meant to amuse, to wound, or to destroy, but to help. He desires excellence.

I would make this point quite clear at the outset, because, having published some of the notes of this book in a weekly paper, I realise from letters which have reached me how very difficult it is for certain individuals to get an unaccustomed notion into their heads. It seems to be a rooted idea with numbers of the public that criticism of Aristocracy is a part of the propaganda of revolution. They cannot distinguish between criticism and abuse; they hold that the remedy for an evil is to hush it up—as if one could hush up a gramophone at an open window. This being the condition of a number of minds, the reader will bear with me, I hope, while I endeavour in a few words to make my purpose perfectly plain.

I am setting out neither to laugh at Fashion, after the manner of the satirists, nor to abuse it, after the manner of political extremists, but to criticise it in the spirit of one who clearly recognises its value to the Commonwealth and would have it faithful to its duties and proud of its privileges.

My standpoint explains everything. It is that of the central classes. I regard the summit of Nobility from the middle-distance of the Gentry. It is in the interests of the entire Commonwealth, but from the position of the central classes, that I criticise the set of people who now occupy the summit of our national life and by their manners and morals create that "climate of opinion" in which we all live. I would persuade these people that they have great duties and great responsibilities; and further I would convince the Gentry that it is their eminent business to see that these people perform those duties and discharge those responsibilities.

By the term Fashion I mean all those noisy, ostentatious, and frivolous people, patricians and plutocrats, politicians and financiers, lawyers and tradesmen, actors and artists, who have scrambled on to the summit of England's national life, and who, setting the worst possible examples in morals and manners, are never so happy as when they are making people talk about them. It is of these ostentatious people I write, and my chief hope is to make the Gentry of England talk about them in such a manner as will either bring them to a sense of their duties or lead to their expulsion from the heights.

Let me persuade timorous people that the social order has much more to fear from the silence of the Gentry in this matter than from the vituperative abuse of the demagogue. The peril of our day is the implication of the Gentry of England in the notorious vulgarity of "all that is fast, furious, and fashionable"; there lies a main opportunity of the social wrecker.

CONTENTS

ILLUSTRATIONS

ANONYMITY

We should be able to use from our hearts
the words which one of Mr. Carlyle's blood-
thirsty heroes spoke with his lips, " Let
our names perish, but the cause prevail " ;
or if we cannot, the sooner we are driven to
this, and are taught to feel that our names
are worth nothing except as they help
forward the cause, the better it will be for
us.   F. D. MAURICE.

What is your opinion of the play ?
Well, who's it by ?
That is a secret for the present.
You don't expect me to know what to
say about a play when I don't know who
the author is, do you ?
                    Fanny's First Play.

THE GLASS OF FASHION

THE GLASS OF FASHION

CHAPTER I

PRINCIPLES OF THE COMMONWEALTH

Friend, call me what you will; no jot care I:
I that shall stand for England till I die.
England!   The England that rejoiced to see
Hellas unbound, Italy one and free;
The England that had tears for Poland's doom,
And in her heart for all the world made room;
The England from whose side I have not swerved,
The Immortal England whom I, too, have served,
Accounting her all living lands above
In Justice, and in Mercy, and in Love.
WILLIAM WATSON.

. . . *No people can be called fully civilised until there is widely diffused among its members the sense of their obligation, not merely to obey the law, but to obey it willingly, and to co-operate in enforcing and maintaining it.*—RAMSAY MUIR.

WHAT is the meaning of England? What is the political value of that name in the world, its significance in the eyes of other nations? Is it possible for us to express in simple language what we feel to be the historical definition of that name, that great name of England, as Henry James has it?

In the spring of 1918, Mr. Alfred Zimmern published an article in *The Round Table* which set before mankind, with a lucidity, a temperance, and a reverence for truth which did not always characterise our war propaganda, the three doctrines which were at that moment in perilous conflict.

> The guns (he said) are still speaking as in 1914, and they will go on speaking, ever more forcibly, till victory is achieved; since, in the great argument which Prussia provoked, no other decision avails.
>
> But side by side with the guns, and mixing its music with theirs, goes a running undercurrent of discussion, of questioning, of philosophising. Men who never reasoned before are turning their minds to consider the cause for which their continued endurance is demanded.

Do not let us forget that endurance; it should underline the definition at which we are attempting to arrive. For the sake of England, let us never cease to remind ourselves, men endured greater horrors than ever before in the history of mankind visited and afflicted the human soul. We might almost say, indeed, that from the days of the Homeric contests down to those burlesque battles of armoured and mounted men in the middle ages, and on to the almost bloodless manœuvres of 1871, war had never existed until 1914. With a higher sensibility than was known to ancient warriors, with a far more delicate nervous organism, and with the greater tenderness of heart which we hope is one of the fruits of British civilisation, young Englishmen were called upon to take part in such a mangling of butchery, such an indiscriminate anarchy of slaughter and mutilation, such a filthiness of Bedlamite carnage, as no man had witnessed from the beginning of time.

And this ordeal was endured in circumstances of the greatest disgust. Separated from their families, torn from their homes, and thrown into the constant and intimate companionship of entire strangers in a foreign land, these English boys lived a life so foreign and unnatural to civilised man that even the shattering sound of the shells came to be reckoned a less evil than the mud of their burrowings, and the loathsome affliction of the lice that preyed upon their bodies.

In such circumstances of horror and disgust the clean youth of England endured the most searching and terrible ordeal to which the human mind has ever been subjected in the whole history of the world, not for a week, not for a month, but for years.

What was it that held them to their posts? "Men who never reasoned before are turning their minds to consider the cause for which their continued endurance is demanded." We may be sure that not many young Englishmen were deluded by the politician's promise of a new England fit for heroes to live in. War had disposed them to be cynical. They had no illusions.

Their reasons were occupied with far other thoughts than those which lend themselves so easily to political rhetoric.   How had this horrible thing come to pass? What had the older people been doing to allow such a calamity to occur?   Was there any escape from this beastliness?

The answer to that last question was universal in the armies of the liberal nations: *No escape till Prussianism is destroyed.*

This feeling was instinctive, rather than rational, but out of it, as the call for endurance continued into the terrible spring of 1918, grew a discussion which enabled the thoughtful English soldier to realise that he was, in sober truth and in the plainest prose, a spiritual warrior.

Men discussed however crudely the three doctrines which Mr. Alfred Zimmern set out so admirably in the pages of *The Round Table* — the doctrine of Prussianism, the doctrine of Bolshevism, and the doctrine of the Commonwealth.   They examined these doctrines and came to a rough conclusion about them.   Prussianism meant political slavery; Bolshevism meant economic slavery; England, with all its faults, meant personal freedom.   It was worth holding out.

With this endurance of our soldiers never absent from our thoughts, let us examine these Three Doctrines as they are now presented to us by Mr. Alfred Zimmern in the collection of his essays entitled *Nationality and Government.*[1]

Prussianism, he reminds us, is no new thing. "You know as well as we do," said the Athenians in 416 B.C. to the representatives of a small people of their day, "that right, as the world goes, is only in question between equals in power, while the strong do what they can, and the weak suffer what they must." Frederick the Great, in the war of the Pragmatic Sanction, was no innovator; how much less was Bethmann-Hollweg original when he made light of treaties and declared that necessity had no law.

Prussianism is a science of government which refuses any relation with ethics. Even as a clever Irishman in the eighties declared that art has no connection with morals, arguing a fallacious thesis so brilliantly that he deceived even many just people, so the philosophers, historians, statesmen, yes, and even in our day the very moralists of Germany, argue that government has no concern with morals.

They remind us of the simple person who inquired concerning the Siamese twins whether they were brothers.

Manifestly, if man is a moral being, he must be moral in all his actions. He cannot be a moral individual, and an immoral official, or an immoral artist, or an immoral tradesman. Morality, that is to say,

[1] *Nationality and Government,* by Alfred Zimmern.

must be of the very stuff and texture of his being, not a decoration for special occasions, or a black coat for Sunday; it must be the soul of the man himself. The German statesman, we may be sure, would complain if his butcher cheated him, and would not listen to the butcher's argument that butchery has nothing to do with ethics. So too, one imagines, the immoral artist would not be satisfied by the excuse of the solicitor who had embezzled his money that the legal profession has no connection with ethics.

But this is to argue with absurdity.

Prussianism, nevertheless, in spite of its manifest absurdity, has a philosophical foundation. It holds that human nature is not to be trusted, that man is born a slave to impulses and caprices which would assuredly ruin him but for the interference and discipline of an iron authority. It sets up that Authority—a machine which takes feeble and defenceless humanity into its cogs — and hammers that dangerous raw material into the disciplined man-power of a mighty State.

The Prussian soldier endured all the horrors endured by the British soldier, and truly fought with a courage which could not be excelled; but his discipline and courage were manufactured for him by a System which uses the slave-owner's instrument of frightfulness and directs itself to human fear.

Prussianism, then, is Authority. But of what nature

is that Authority? It is the Authority of a Materialism which denies morality, the Authority of National-
ism, Self-Assertion, Conquest, and Brutality. To the
Prussian the individual has neither dignity nor rights
outside his State. The State is everything; the individual is its slave. But the individual, in order to
serve the State, must not be neglected—he must be
cultivated and equipped for the discharge of his duties.
Hence Prussianism has taken the great and sacred
weapon of knowledge, and made it serve an evil purpose.
The people of Germany are educated and trained as
no other people in the world. Mentally they have
no superiors. But in character they are inferior to the
least of the nations, and the worst of them are on a level
with savages. It is not Authority that is responsible
for this mass destruction, but the nature of the Authority. Prussianism is Machinery. It is brain, not
character. It is the State, not Man.

Bolshevism, as Mr. Zimmern says, is akin to
Prussianism. It is a religion founded in violence,
and inspired by contempt of individual freedom. It
distrusts the human race; it hates the human soul.
By terror and by ruthless force, humanity is to be
shackled to the tumbril of an economic theory. It
is not a new thing; it is as old as slavery. Mr. Bertrand Russell, in the ablest book yet published on the
Russian Revolution, and the most persuasive because
the most honest, outspoken, and courageous, shows to

all those who have eyes to see that beneath the verbiage
of Lenin and beneath the communistic mask of Trotsky
there is in truth nothing more original than the hideous
features of despotism and tyranny.

The Englishman sees with clearness that neither the
doctrine of Prussianism nor the doctrine of Bolshevism
squares with his inherent notions of the purposes of
existence. He has freedom in his blood, and a long
tradition of common sense in his mind. England by no
means fulfils at present his ideal of a commonwealth,
but it is on the right road, a road at any rate which
leads onward, not a side turning which ends in a cul-de-
sac. He prefers to march onward as a free man rather
than to find himself trapped by a tyranny. Prussianism
is not yet destroyed. It has its votaries in this country,
just as Bolshevism has; and for the next few years the
conflict between these two doctrines and the doctrine of
the Commonwealth will be fought out in discussions of
various kinds on English soil. It is a good thing that
this should be so, for truth has no fear of an open conflict
with error.

Let us see how the doctrine of the Commonwealth,
the English principle, compares with these two doctrines
which are so similar in spirit and both of which are so
fatal to the higher life of the human race.

Mr. Zimmern, comparing our methods of education
with the German, quotes the opening words of the
English Code:

The purpose of the Public Elementary School is to form and strengthen the character and to develop the intelligence of the children entrusted to it.

First character, then intelligence. This order goes to the very heart of the difference between the principle of Prussianism and the principle of the Commonwealth.

The Prussian system is unsatisfactory, firstly, because *it confuses external discipline with self-control;* secondly, because *it confuses regimentation with corporate spirit;* thirdly, because *it conceives the nation's duty in terms of "culture" rather than of character.*

"Our British tendency," continues Mr. Zimmern, "is to develop habits of service and responsibility through a devotion to smaller and more intimate associations, to build on a foundation of lesser loyalties and duties. We do not conceive it to be the function of the school to *teach* patriotism or to *teach* fellowship.

Rather we hold that good education *is* fellowship, *is* citizenship, in the deepest meaning of those words. . . . A school, a ship, a club, a Trade Union, any free association of Englishmen, is all England in miniature."

With us, he points out, civilisation stands for neither language nor culture nor anything intellectual at all. *"It stands for something moral and social and political"*:

It means, in the first place, the establishment and enforcement of the Rule of Law, as against anarchy on the one hand and tyranny on the other; and secondly, on the basis of order and justice, the task of making men fit for free institutions, the work of guiding and training them to recognise the obligations of citizenship, to subordinate their own personal interests or inclinations to the common welfare, the "commonwealth."

In a word it means Character, not a national character, but an individual moral character. Our common sense has taught us that the most important thing about a man is his verity. We are not to be put off by smooth speeches or an imposing manner; we go to the heart of things and ask what is the character of this man who would traffic with us or sit down with our family at dinner. Is he a man to be trusted? Is he straight? Is he clean? Or is he a humbug, a rogue, and a hypocrite?

Mr. Chesterton, with his robust love of beer and incense, has attempted to make light of the age of the Puritans; but he is obliged to confess that in the simpler Puritans there was a "ring of real republican virtue," and "a defiance of tyrants," and also, which is the greatest of all his own affirmations, "an assertion of human dignity." Is it not plain to us, whatever their theological extravagances may have been, that because their insistence was on moral character these men were the essential English of that period? In comparison with them, surely the courtiers and fops who surrounded Charles II were as little English as the Euphuists of Elizabethan times or the alien financiers of our present Belgravia.

The Puritan's face was set against licence. He

hated anything that degraded the human spirit. His moral emphasis was on the inner life—the inward verity of the individual. He raised morality from a matter of taste to a rule of life, to a test of value. He was for honesty, not duplicity; for worth, not pretentiousness; for chastity, not beastliness; for the home, not the brothel; for manliness, not effeminacy. If he lacked Mr. Chesterton's passion for symbolism, did he not also lack the treachery of Charles I, the licentiousness of Charles II? Was there not essential Englishness in the challenge of Richard Sibbes: "What are we to think of those who would bring light and darkness, Christ and Anti-Christ, the Ark and Dagon together, that would reconcile us *as if it were no great matter?*" We owe something to the brilliant wit of Mr. Chesterton, but how much more to the moral earnestness of Milton.

It was the Puritan who carried English character across the Atlantic, and founded the mightiest republic the world has known—a republic still in its infancy, but, with England, the world's greatest bulwark at this hour against tyranny of every kind, whether the tyranny of the priest, the monarch, or the communist. In the light of that tremendous achievement, is it not just to say that the Calvinism of which Mr. Chesterton makes so much was merely the theological accident of the time, and that the true passion of the Puritan, distinguishing him from the false and traitorous English of that day, and enabling him to do this mighty work in America, was the passion for liberty, for moral earnestness, for the dignity of the individual?

Prussianism rests, as Bismarck, a moderate man, asserted in memorable words, on the divine right of the King of Prussia. Has Mr. Chesterton, who hates Prussianism, forgotten that James I of England wrote to his son, afterwards Charles I, bidding him remember, "God made you a little GOD, to sit on His Throne, and rule over men." Against that doctrine the Puritan first protested and then fought, so saving England from a tyranny which would infallibly have destroyed her moral character.

It was the true descendant of this Puritan, we may say faithfully, who defeated the Prussian tyranny, for the ranks of the British Army were filled with millions of volunteers who fought for the principle of the Commonwealth, and who endured the incredible agony of that long conflict because they hated despotism, and felt in their English blood something that would not bow to an Authority against which their moral nature revolted.

If the record of the British Commonwealth under the stress of war (wrote Mr. Zimmern) is less resounding than the martial bulletins of Prussia, less stirring and fantastic than the sweeping edicts of the revolution, if its plans and achievements are dressed in the sober tints of ordinary life, it is because the Commonwealth exists not to gratify a conqueror's ambition or to demonstrate or refute a dreamer's doctrine, but to enable its citizens to grow to the full stature of their moral being.

Not by the triumphs of the battlefield and the forum will the Commonwealth seek to be justified, but by the character and the influence, the noble example and the inspiring memory of its men and women.

That is to say, the meaning of England is neither Imperialism nor State Slavery, but Moral Character. She is the very antithesis of Prussianism, and the very antipodes of Bolshevism. Her strength, power, and dominion lie in no machinery of State, but in the moral character of her individual citizens.

These things I have set down in order that the reader may carry in his mind a clear idea of the meaning of England as he proceeds to examine her social documents of the present hour.

England, still far short of her ideal, stands in a world of many diverse doctrines, and a world at many different levels of civilisation, for Liberty and Character. She means that human nature is a great thing, not a slavish thing, a potentiality, at any rate, which may be educated in self-control, till it is fit to stand on its own feet against all the assaults of the world, the flesh, and the devil. She utters an Everlasting No to the tyrant who would substitute external discipline for self-control, regimentation for corporate spirit, and "culture" for character. She utters this Everlasting No to tyrants of every kind, whether it be the Prussian who would make the citizen exist for the State, or the Bolshevist who would make the worker exist for Economics.

And from her heart of hearts she utters an Everlasting Yea to the divine demand of religion for truth in the inward parts.

She stands, then, for something infinitely great. It is vital to the higher life of the human race that she should continue to stand for this great thing, since tyranny never sleeps, and the victory for Freedom will not be won till all nations have acquired the moral character which renders liberty a power and not a danger.

The question we now have to ask ourselves is whether those people in England who set the nation its standards in morals and manners are helping us to stand for this great thing, are strengthening our moral fibres and quickening our spiritual ideals, or whether they are leading the nation into an ambush where tyranny waits to strike another blow at his chief enemy.

It is not a question, I beg the reader to remember, whether Fashion is worse than it was, or better; it is a question whether it is a help or a hindrance, whether it is adequate to the present crisis in the fortunes of civilisation.

LADY HARROWBY

CHAPTER II

COLONEL REPINGTON'S DIARIES

We have neither immediate nor remote aims, and in our soul there is a great empty space.—Anton Tchehov.

Wilhelm von Humboldt, one of the most beautiful souls that have ever existed, used to say that one's business in life was first to perfect oneself by all the means in one's power, and secondly to try to create in the world around one an aristocracy, the most numerous that one possibly could, of talents and characters.—Matthew Arnold.

In order to avoid any charge of vagueness or extravagance, which is the usual defence in matters of this nature, I propose to test Fashionable Society only by its own documents. The documents I shall use are the recent published work of fashionable people, and give us valuable information concerning a great number of other fashionable people. They have been published without shame, have achieved a considerable popularity, and are acknowledged by the best judges to be thoroughly indiscreet—that is to say, truthful but unwise.

There shall be no opportunity for the timorous sycophant of Fashion to dismiss my indictment as any mere essay in vulgar sensationalism.   I look to startle people; I hope to rouse anger and indignation among the solid central classes of England; but the means I shall employ to that end are no fabrications of my own, no exaggerations of a gossip's chatter, no scraps and pickings from the refuse heaps of scandal; they are the signed and written word of people who live at the very centre of fashionable life and who are wholly above suspicion as enemies of the social order.

Since I earnestly desire the reader to keep the War in his mind, and to remember my suggestion that our soldiers endured the inexpressible torture of that ordeal for the sake of a great moral, social, and political ideal— the ideal of the British Commonwealth—we will begin with Colonel Charles à Court Repington, C.M.G., Commander of the Order of Leopold, Officer of the Legion of Honour, and author of *The First World War*.[1]

Colonel Repington is a man of intellect—an admirable and finished specimen of the intellectual man of the world.   His vanity, which leaves Malvolio at the post, must not blind us to the reality of his services during the War.   He rendered this country very considerable services, for which we must ever pay him the tribute of a profound gratitude.   His military knowledge, which is of a high order, his manners, which can be exceedingly engaging, and his courage, which is

[1] *The First World War.*

proof against the airs and tempers of men in high places, faithfully and persistently served this country and this country's allies at every crisis in the War. I think I am right in saying that only in one military particular was his judgment ever at fault, and that never once did he consult his own leisure or convenience when a long and racking journey, with a difficult diplomatic mission at the end of it, was likely to retrieve the mistakes of our politicians and serve the safety of our troops.

Colonel Repington's two volumes are the contents of his diaries from 1914 to 1918. At the outbreak of War he was fifty-six years of age, had seen service in Afghanistan, Burma, Egypt, and South Africa, had served as military attaché in Belgium and Holland, was military correspondent to *The Times*, a popular figure in the drawing-rooms of London and Paris, and a man whose opinion on military subjects was listened to with respect by many of our greatest soldiers and some of our most intellectual statesmen.

In him we see the product of all the social advantages. Born of the aristocracy, educated at Eton, always associating on terms of the friendliest intimacy with the great and powerful, a traveller who would have astonished the Elizabethans, an excellent linguist, a man of taste and judgment, a sportsman in the best English sense of that word, and a sincere lover of the beautiful, Colonel Repington comes before us with every hall-mark of aristocratic genuineness, so blest by the gods, for he is a singularly handsome person, that a former generation might have taken him for the ideal hero of a Ouida novel.

Might we not reasonably expect to find, then, in the war diaries of a man so blest and so circumstanced, a spirit that would help us to penetrate to the heart of that moral idealism which held our soldiers to their post? If Colonel Repington does not know what England stood for in the War, how shall the man know who has read only the elements of history, and since that day has been too busy earning his bread to cultivate his mind? And if Colonel Repington does know what England stood for in that conflict, should not the diaries he filled during those dreadful years tell us as few other documents of the time could do how the great ideal of England sustained English aristocracy through that long conflict and led it to such shining sacrifices as made that ideal manifest to all the world?

I do not think it is unreasonable to expect such a spirit in these diaries. The times were tremendous. Civilisation, as the noblest minds of the human race have ever understood that term, was in peril. There were crises when it seemed that nothing could save the young liberalism of Europe. For months many abandoned hope that Prussian despotism, Prussian materialism, Prussian savagery, could even be held, much less overthrown. Think what that meant; control was conquering—self-control was fighting with its back to the wall.   An iron hand was closing over the soul of freedom.   A grasp of slavery like that which now holds Russia in its ruthless clutches was tightening round the writhing body of this world's liberty.   And during those months of almost unendurable suspense the flower of England's youth was bleeding to death in the most frightful shambles that even a maniac could imagine.   It was no nightmare.   The thing was real. It was not the campaign of Cæsar, Charlemagne, Frederick, or Napoleon; it was not a campaign far off and distant; it was a campaign at our very door; and that battered door was being defended by our brothers and our sons.   Not by the hundred, or by the thousand, or by the score of thousands, but by hundreds of thousands; yes, and in the end by *millions*, men were being killed, mutilated, blinded, and driven mad, *then*, at that moment, in those very days, when Colonel Repington was filling his diaries.

Most people felt this agony in their blood.   It was something from which there was no escape.   It was as close to life as the skin to the body.   To know that freedom was in peril, and that it was being bloodily and awfully defended by boys fresh from school, was a mental experience which could not be dislodged.   To shake off the intolerable burden of that thought for a few moments was possible; diversion was even necessary to health; it was right, it was just; but to wish to forget it altogether, this was criminal; and to write about the

War without the consecration of that thought always in the mind, to make the War the theme of two volumes, and never once write one single word suggesting even a consciousness of that holy thought, the Cause for which our men were fighting, this, until I read Colonel Repington's work, I should have said was impossible.

To read these volumes is to discover the unthinkable and the impossible. Nowhere will you find a period or a sentence of which you could say, *"There! that is what we fought for!"* The Cause finds no expression. There is no penetration to the spiritual reality of the conflict. It never seems to have occurred to the author that the soldier in the trenches might have preferred "the trivial detail of daily happiness" to War, but for something that held him there like a priest at the altar.

Colonel Repington met everybody. He sets down in his diary what he said to those great people, and also what the great people said to him. They were our greatest, and apparently not one word was uttered which ever glanced below the surface. A Frenchman might read this book and exclaim of us, "What cynics!" or a German, and say, "What hypocrites!" or an educated Indian, and say, "What animals!" No one reading this book would understand that England was fighting for the greatest political ideal which has ever risen from the furnace of slavery, and that her sons were offering their lives in no less a cause than the higher life of the human race.

Never was book written with greater omission. Bagehot censured Scott for the entire omission from his novels of an "element which is so characteristic of life," religion; but who could write a book about the First World War and omit the cause which, if challenged by a Second, will surely perish? It is as if the armies of the world were fighting for a bone.

But if we censure Colonel Repington for this grave omission, what must we say of the incidents, the anecdotes, the conversations, and the flippancies which crowd his two volumes from cover to cover? Take, for example, this entry in the diaries under the head "The Outlook for 1916":

Lunched in Belgrave Square. Lady Paget, Prince and Princess Victor Napoleon, Mrs. Duggan, Wolkoff, and Max Müller, of the Foreign Office. The Princess very nicely dressed, and charming as usual. Mrs. Duggan was in the most attractive widow's weeds imaginable. Callaud (*sic*) of Paris makes a speciality of mourning for war widows apparently. These particular weeds included a very pretty hat in crape, with a veil hanging down behind, or rather streamers, and a narrow band of white crape round the hat next her face, and also under her chin. The dress had a white waistcoat of tulle, and open at the neck, in fact she looked like a fascinating nun. Laszlo has painted her in this dress.

One is not only shocked by such an entry, but filled with a dull nausea. Something is here degraded which, for most of us, has the elements of sanctity.

Such a spirit is here forced before our attention as would admit the cinematograph to the death-chamber.

Apparently, Colonel Repington and his friends were occasionally visited by the disturbing thought that their lives were scarcely in harmony with the tragic character of the times. On one occasion at least this intrusive thought was faced and challenged with a characteristic logic:

> Lady Ridley and I discussed what posterity would think of us in England. We agreed that we should be considered rather callous to go on with our usual life when we were reading of 3,000 and 4,000 casualties a day. But she said that people could not keep themselves elevated permanently on some plane above the normal, and she supposed that things round us explained the French Revolution and the behaviour of the French nobility.

This entry, in spite of its brittle fallacy, is valuable. It acts as a finger-post to "the usual life" which Fashion considers normal. In the next chapter we will follow that direction and see where it leads us.

For the moment, apologising to the intelligent reader for wasting his time, I would point out to those who agree with Lady Ridley that her excuse is on all fours with the excuse made by the most degraded people in our social hotch-potch for their horrible morals and their disgusting manners.

The prostitute does not think of herself as abnormal; on the contrary, she regards modesty and chastity as unnatural elevations above the plane of the normal. The crowd of rascals and scoundrels who infest the Turf do not think of themselves as "rather callous" or as savages utterly unfit for civilisation; on the contrary, they regard honesty, straight dealing, and the most elementary self-sacrifice as elevations fantastically and laughably above the plane of the normal.

If "the normal" is to be at the sport of individual caprice, the life of a community can never escape from chaos. There must be standards. There must be criteria. The tendency to regard loyalty to one's lower nature as honesty, and all moral strivings to obey the whispers of one's higher nature as hyprocrisy, is fatal to development, fatal to order. The aim must be at perfection. The standards of humanity must be delivered into our hands by the highest.

How disastrously any other principle works may be seen in this extract from Colonel Repington's diary for February 26, 1918:

Lady Randolph and I agree that if we began again at 17 we should do the same as we had done, only more so. Then we decided that we could not have done more so if we had tried.

The manner is flippant, but the spirit is unmistakable. It is the fatal spirit of self-satisfaction. Beneath all their frivolity and trivial persiflage, these people are profoundly convinced of superiority, profoundly unaware of unworthiness. *They have no idea of their guilt.* Their privileges appear to them as the fruits of their merits, and their merits seem to them so unquestionable as to be a full discharge of their responsibilities. They think the rest of mankind should be grateful to them for their mere existence. That horrible creature Lady Cardigan speaks of someone having to earn her living as a governess "instead of enjoying the life her birth and attractions merited." *Noblesse oblige.* As the tout of the race-course laughs at the tract of the missionary, so these people who ought to quicken the nation's sense of its duties, and who ought to set the community the highest standards of moral perfection, laugh at such an utterance of Matthew Arnold: "The deeper I go in my own consciousness, and the more simply I abandon myself to it, the more it seems to tell me that I have no rights at all, only duties."

But conscience is the least obtrusive of visitors in these circles. When "the normal" is being fixed, convenience, not conscience, is the arbiter.

CHAPTER III

SOME GLIMPSES OF THE NORMAL

What bothered me in London was all the Clever People going wrong with such Clever Reasons for so doing, which I couldn't confute.—EDWARD FITZGERALD.

Each London season is as like the past as this year's turnip crop is like last. . . . One wearies of the energetic monotony which teaches one nothing and loses its power to amuse.—J. A. FROUDE.

WITH so admirable a guide for our purpose as the famous and intellectual Colonel Repington, we will set out to discover the normal life of fashionable people. That is to say, we will listen to the voice of Fashion while she tells us what she likes to talk about at her meals, what she considers amusing, what interests her in life, what she thinks of all those great subjects which occupy the thoughts of serious men, and what spirit animates her social round.

I am not seeking to fasten a charge of iniquity on Fashion, but to discover its *atmosphere*.

In perusing these following extracts from Colonel Repington's diaries, I would remind the reader that

27

only on the rarest occasions does the name of a New
Rich person occur in those pages; therefore he may be
assured in his mind that he is reading of those who by
birth, tradition, and all the advantages of education are
entitled to set the nation its moral and social standards:

> We all agreed upon the desirability of cheering up
> and lighting up London; having restaurant cars on trains,
> holding exhibitions, and emulating the French coolness,
> instead of remaining gloomy in sackcloth and ashes as
> *The Times* has advocated.   They want me to move in
> the matter.   Mrs. Duggan looking very pretty, and her
> mourning is growing less.

I need scarcely interrupt the guidance of Colonel
Repington to inform the reader that *The Times* did
not advocate "sackcloth and ashes," but I would
point out the significance of that playful phrase, since
it so obviously suggests that Fashion regards dignity
and decency in the light of undertakers, or, as the slang
of the day has it, kill-joys.   This dislike of anything
in the nature of spiritual dignity or intellectual seriousness is a marked characteristic of fashionable psychology.
The reader will encounter this spirit in many of the
extracts I shall make from the documents of Fashion
in the course of these pages:

> We discussed some lighter subjects, including the
> Kaiser's pet ladies, of whom he seems to possess types in
> Norway, Venice, etc., as well as in Brussels.   The P.M.
> (Mr. Lloyd George) much enjoyed this gossip, and his
> eyes twinkled as he listened to it.

The following entry appears under the date *Good Friday, April 21, 1916:*

We had tennis, fishing, walking, bridge, charades, music and games, and fooling of every description. . . . We had a most cheery party, and were all very friendly and young. A capable cook and a good cellar did no harm. With Ross, Rumbold, and the two dancing ladies to act for us, and with Wolkoff at the piano, the evenings passed very pleasantly. Ross is a great loss to low comedy. . . .

We had forgathered to talk German politics, but got on to ladies and horses, and soon forgot all about the Boches.

We discussed the vices and virtues of man and woman. Lady R. said that no woman ever loved a good man, and Juliet agreed, saying that it was the last thing that gave any satisfaction. Lady R. said that man had terrible advantages over woman, as he came into the cradle fully armed. I said that the woman did, too, but I was howled down. Lady Cunard thought that a woman ought to have romance and a man a sense of humour, and then we tried to define what a sense of humour was, and on going round the table we found that everyone thought they had it.

Here follows one of the most amazing entries in Colonel Repington's diaries. The amazement lies in the fact that the remark recorded was made in the presence of a mother and her sons:

Dined with Belle Herbert and her two boys, Sidney and Michael, and Juliet Duff, in Carlton House Terrace. A very pleasant evening. They screamed over my story of Robertson's remark that he and I could no more afford to be seen walking together just now than we could afford to be seen walking down Regent Street with a whore.

I confess that while I am fairly used to a rather brutal vigour of language among certain men of fashion, I have never in my life heard such an expression as this in the company of women. Nor do I think that "screaming" is a usual form of laughter among even fashionable women.

Here, too, is an amazing story to be told in the circles of refinement and culture:

> The other story was of Harry Higgins and a famous beautiful prima donna. Harry was trying to engage her for the opera and she held out for £200 a night. "But we only want you to *sing*, you know," rasped out Harry in her ear.

"Ragging" appears from time to time in these *souvenirs d'enfance:*

> A very cheery evening. We dressed up in the hats from the crackers, ragged a good deal, went out into the square at midnight to hear the chimes, and then back to drink an excellent punch and sing "Auld Lang Syne."
> Some good tennis, much talk and much bridge. In the evening a great rag. We got to bed about 3 a.m., and the next night was almost as bad, if not worse.

"The next night" was Sunday.

I do not pretend to know the nature of the "rags" which are mentioned occasionally, but never described, in these pages. Readers of Mr. Michael Sadleir's novel *Privilege* will know that in some sets at any rate they take a very horrible form.   Mr. Wilfrid Blunt mentions a pretty dreadful incident of the kind in *My Diaries*, Part II., that extraordinary work which more than confirms every word I wrote about Mr. Asquith and Mr. Arthur Balfour in *The Mirrors of Downing Street*. But I prefer to think that the rags of Colonel Repington are merely foolish, like the rags in a very exalted circle, where pulling out the ties of men in a ball-room seems to afford the greatest possible amusement to gentlemen in a highly responsible position.   Horseplay is the chief note of the modern rag. Girls are chased about a house by young men, upstairs and downstairs, and sometimes come in for such a clawing as quite ruins their garments.   There are minor rags, hardly perhaps to be called rags, in which eccentricity plays the chief part.   Colonel Repington speaks of a house occupied by Mrs. Asquith at Bognor, which could hold eight people, but into which Mrs. Asquith thought nothing of squeezing eighteen; at this house Lady Diana Manners came to stay, and insisted, we are told, on midnight bathing.

The baths have a fine assortment of salts and ointments and scented waters for the bathers to select from.   This reminded Mrs. McKenna of Lord D'Abernon, who says that when he stays with a Jew he always pours the whole of the bath salts into his tub as a protest against the Crucifixion.

We discussed Irvingites, taxation, tanks, the War generally, and other matters, Lady C. occasionally throwing in her usual impromptu and startling observations such as that Balfour was an abstraction and not a man, and that the *upper* part of his face was like Christ—which made A. J. B. laugh consumedly.

With one other extract from Colonel Repington's pages, I will leave the exploration of his book, which has many merits, to the reader who cares to compare my few samples with the thing as a whole.

This particular extract brings us back to the War. The date is September, 1917, the place Paris:

Le Roy asked me the inevitable question about the end of the War, and I said that I saw no good reason why it should end until the Huns were more badly beaten. Since nations counted money no more than pebbles on a beach, and all would probably repudiate in one form or another at the end of the War, there seemed no reason for stopping, especially as so many people were growing rich by the War; the ladies liked being without their husbands, and all dreaded the settlement afterwards, industrial, political, financial, domestic.

In this paragraph of the diarist you may discover, I think, the germ of that disease which has destroyed the moral character of modern Fashion: the disease, I mean, of cynicism. The living principle of a cynical spirit is scepticism, but scepticism only of what is high and honourable, sincere and true, virtuous and earnest. As touching all that is low, abominable, contemptible,

LORD MORLEY

disgusting, cowardly, or disgraceful to a man of principle, cynicism is credulity itself.

People like Colonel Repington know as well as we do that no great nation would repudiate its debt unless actual ruin brought the whole financial structure of its civilisation to the dust. They know, too, that for thousands of women the absence of their husbands in the War was an intolerable anguish, calling from their lips night after night, and morning after morning, such prayers as Amelia in Brussels addressed to God for the safety of George Osborne. They know these things as well as we do; in the privacy of their hearts they acknowledge them; but to admit such opinions in public, to state them in print, to publish them with their names to the world, this would do violence to the essential scepticism of their souls, and worse, damage their reputations in fashionable circles as men and women of the world.

The normal life of these people is governed by cynicism. In their horror of enthusiasm, which they regard as vulgar, they have fallen into the pit of sneers. They like to depreciate; it is natural to them to degrade. The universe has no majesty for them, life no secrets, religion no reverence, and the nature of man no illusions. They know everything—everything that darkens and destroys, nothing that elevates, nothing that purifies, nothing that sustains.

It is from this normal life, this shallow life of the

3

spiritual depths, that Fashion finds it impossible permanently to elevate itself. It cannot take generous views. It cannot cherish noble faiths. It cannot strive. To climb to the heights, to direct the vision to the morning star, to lead the way to greater truth, greater beauty, and greater goodness, this would be too exhausting for souls enervated, if not rotted, by the negations of cynicism. From such people, is it not unreasonable to expect guidance and direction? In such hands as these, can we expect to see the standards of the higher life of the human race held above the battlefields of the soul? From such lips do we expect to hear the oracles of wisdom above the clamours and violence of political change?

"An age that is ceasing to produce child-like children," said Francis Thompson, "cannot produce a Shelley." And he asked society:

Know you what it is to be a child? It is to be something very different from the man of to-day. It is to have a spirit yet streaming from the waters of baptism; it is to believe in love, to believe in loveliness, to believe in belief . . . it is

To see a world in a grain of sand,
And a heaven in a wild flower,
Hold infinity in the palm of your hand,
And eternity in an hour.

It is to know not as yet that you are under sentence of life, nor petition that it be commuted into death.

How discordantly this extract rings in the company of quotations from *The First World War!* One feels that it has the uncouth Doric of a solecism. One knows that Fashion will raise her darkened eyebrows at it.

If we have discovered the normal life of Fashion, and if we wish to strengthen England's place in the world, we must ask ourselves whether that normal life is helpful or destructive. Fashion may not intend it, but her normal life descends to lower levels, and pervades the entire organism of the State. Therefore her example is a serious matter; for those who care for England, and believe in her destiny, it is a vital matter.

The question, then, that such people who care for England have to ask themselves is a simple one. It is whether cynicism is right. If right, then it is good for all classes of the community. It is good for the Bolshevist. But if wrong, it is treason in the high places of the State, that and nothing less.

One way of discovering whether an idea is right is to see how it works. Let us ask ourselves, then, if the philosophy of cynicism works in fashionable circles. Are these people useful? Are they happy? Do they make us feel that life is worth living?

If we see that these people are not useful; if we discover that they are not happy; if we know in our hearts that they have no encouragement to give to moral earnestness, intellectual striving, spiritual aspiration, or even physical effort; if we find them to be the wreckage of the human spirit miserably dragging the chain of their days from the tents of Vanity Fair to the wilderness of disillusion; then, truly, we can do the State great service merely by removing these false captains from the conspicuous van of English civilisation. They may be the victims of circumstances; properly known they may be objects for our compassion; but while they march at the head of the nation they are, first of all things, our enemies.

CHAPTER IV

MRS. ASQUITH'S AUTOBIOGRAPHY

Oh, my God, that you won't listen to a woman of quality when her heart is bursting!—VANBRUGH.

FROM the document of a man of the world we will now turn to the document of a woman of the world—*The Autobiography of Margot Asquith.*[1]

Mrs. Asquith belongs to that insurgent class of the commercial rich which broke into society soon after the second Reform Bill, and during the years of King Edward's reign completely overwhelmed it. She is the more deadly foe to our ancient traditions because her attack is not aimed at the primitive virtues of humanity—those moral outworks of the social organism. She does not come up against morals charioted by Bacchus and his pards; she is certainly no Laïs reeling forward in the social route to clink goblets with Silenus, no anarchist of conduct who would carve "Do as you like" across humanity's immemorial tables of stone. On the contrary, she is a devoted wife, an exemplary mother, and she believes in God.

[1] *The Autobiography of Margot Asquith.*

Her attack is the more fatal, because it is aimed from the cherished centre of domestic life. It is in my view, whether she is conscious of it or not, an attack upon manners. That is to say, it is not an attack upon the moral law, but upon the manner in which that law should be handled. She breaks no commandments, but will not keep them within "the bounds of decency." Nature would appear to have fashioned her with a thirst for self-expression so burning, so gritted with the sand of a spiritual Sahara, that she could not brook the ancient limitations with which the wisdom of society long ago hedged about the development of character.

The path into which her disposition urged her appears to have been the path of sensationalism. To attract attention to herself she converted her share of the hidden river of life into a fountain that should never cease to play—if you will, into a burst water pipe. To be taken for a personality she had to be different from other people. If the world went on its way, carrying the taper of modesty through the darkness of this human night, she would pin Catherine wheels to her front, fasten a Roman candle at her brow, and advance brandishing a rocket in either hand. In other words, Mrs. Asquith seems to me from the evidence of these pages deliberately to have sought notoriety by shock tactics. She has arrived at the wall by trampling down the flowers.

She seems to have flung herself quite early in life

against society's spiritual paling of modesty, self-effacement, restraint, and delicacy.   She broke through it completely in the dawn of her womanhood.   Since then, arrived on the once sacred summit, she appears to have lent a sturdy hand to the building of that Tower of Babel which is now lighted by so many winking electric signs that it remains in the public eye even at night. She is, decisively and victoriously, of the company known as People Who Are Talked About.

Now, to some it may seem that this is to bring a charge against the lady in language too severe for the offence.   After all (one supposes them to say), is it not natural for a high-spirited girl to desire attention? And is *l'enfant terrible* to be regarded as a criminal directly she puts up her hair and lets down her skirt?

This objection shows only the dangerous pass to which people of Mrs. Asquith's description have brought the public judgment.   Tolerance, said Coleridge, is only possible when indifference has made it so.

Immodesty is not one of the smaller sins; it is almost the greatest.   To be loud, to be ostentatious, to be always thinking of self-expression, is not to find a policeman approaching us, but to empty the heart of its divinest essence.   If a vulgar audacity, a constant daring, a ceaseless pushfulness of the soul, fill us with no horror, it is because we have become indifferent to the spiritual life.   Nothing, indeed, so insidiously corrupts the spiritual foundations of human character as that intemperate egoism which looks with contempt upon modesty, and nothing can be more fatal to society. We can wait for a gross aristocracy to come to its repentant senses in its next generation. But what is to be the end of an English aristocracy which decides for anarchy in manners? Better to go honestly to the trough than to sit painting one's face at an open window.

If you would understand quite clearly what I mean, compare Lord Frederic Hamilton's picture of his mother, the gracious and beautiful Duchess of Abercorn, with the looking-glass portrait of Mrs. Asquith's autobiography. The duchess belonged to a society which had no acquaintance with the Vulgar Rich. One may say of her that she did not avoid limelight, but that she had no knowledge of its existence. She was not only exemplary in all the relations of human life, but she possessed, like Mme. Roland, "a consummate moral nature"; and, like Mme. Guizot, aimed at "an inner development of integrity, delicacy, refinement of thought, and refinement of feeling." Her exquisite manners were the outward and visible expression of a vital inward and spiritual grace.

She could not have written such a book as this. The idea is inconceivable. Even if she had been brought to direst penury she could not have sold to the public the story of her love. Far rather would she have died of starvation. But Mrs. Asquith sells to the public not merely the long chronicle of her amorous adventures, telling us who proposed to her and how she explained matters to the first Mrs. Asquith, but even a most intimate letter of sympathy written to her, by a man still living, on the death of one of her children.

What are we to think of such insensibility as this? Here, of course, she was not thinking of sensation; a monetary incentive must have been not merely far from her thoughts but obliterated from her mind.   Yet the sacred letter goes in with the rest.   How was this possible?

We ask ourselves, did no tears fall upon it?   Did her hand not shake a little when she turned over the fading pages, remembering the acuteness of her former anguish?   Did she not shrink, if only for a moment, from the profanation of giving those words, which had meant so much to her, to the printer?   All we know is this, that the letter went in with the rest.

Yet we read, "I shrank then, as I do now, from exposing the secrets and sensations of life.   Reticence should guard the soul, and only those who have compassion should be admitted to the shrine.   When I peer among my dead or survey my living friends, I see hardly anyone with this quality."   Notice that word *peer*.

Surely there is in this paragraph evidence of a mind too heated and disordered for clear thinking.   The lady sorrowfully puts friendship on one side, and dances away to embrace the printer.

Do not let us hurry past this disagreeable incident.

Is it not a just conclusion that Mrs. Asquith gave this letter to the publisher because she could see no harm in that action? And if she saw no harm in it, must we not therefore conclude that she does not feel the same compunctions which operate in almost all civilised persons? But she is moral, clever, brave, kind. She is no monster. How, then, is it that she did not feel those compunctions?

The answer is—she has ceased to be simple.

This is the peril of aristocracy, the most deadly blow inflicted upon it by the forces which have conquered and possessed its territory. All beauty of the heart, all grandeur of the mind, all dignity of the spirit, repose upon the first simplicities of human nature, the pieties which were as natural to Newton and Wordsworth as to any of those Suffolk old women with whose cottage talk Edward FitzGerald was wont to refresh his spirit after visiting London.

There was a time when English aristocracy made its influence felt throughout the whole social organism from a privacy and a seclusion which were inviolate. Queen Victoria's great duchesses of Abercorn, Buccleuch, Sutherland, Devonshire, Marlborough, and Westminster; the Cecils, the Lytteltons, and the Greys; women like Lady Frederick Cavendish and George Wyndham's mother, these radiated through the national life a spiritual influence which had its source in the simplicities of the human heart. That time is past

We are a nation without standards.   Society's door has been opened from within, and we now look through that portal upon a spectacle which, where it does not disgust, either baffles us or bores us with ennui.

We could not have a better witness to this truth than Mrs. Asquith.   She is not evil; she is not base; she is by no means without good qualities.   But how disastrously she has lost her way!   Observe that she does not know when she offends good taste.   She is terribly immodest without being aware of it.   She dances before us, grimaces, curtsies, kisses her hand to the public, without any fear that many may laugh and some may turn away with a shudder.   She seems to be an illustration of a derisive phrase in the north, "an owd yow dressed lamb fashion."   Spiritually she has not grown; she is still in the nursery; her greatest happiness is still to be brought downstairs after dinner to amuse the guests.   Time has not developed her finer qualities; it has only intensified her worst.

Amiel says of people who snatch their hands away from Simplicity, and go their own way to predominance and power:

> . . . they do not live by the soul; they ignore the immutable and eternal; they bustle at the circumference of their existence because they cannot penetrate to its centre.   They are restless, eager, positive, because they are superficial.   To what end, all this stir, noise, greed, struggle?   It is all a mere being stunned and deafened.

Lessing said: "Ever so much lightning does not make daylight."

Mrs. Asquith reminds me in one respect of Mme. de Staël, who was so restless for a sceptre that she kept a twig of laurel by her side with which she toyed during conversation. How she fought against the advancing years "which echo with hoarse voice the brilliant airs of youth!" Moreover, when she lay dying, she had herself carried out into the garden and there distributed roses for remembrance. The penalty of ceasing to be simple is that we become theatrical.

In order that the reader who has not yet possessed himself of Mrs. Asquith's *Autobiography* may see Fashionable Society from her angle, as he has already seen it from Colonel Repington's, I will give a few extracts from her pages:

> Laura had been disturbed by hearing that we were considered "fast." She told me that receiving company in our bedroom shocked people and that we ought, perhaps, to give it up. I listened closely to what she had to say and at the end remarked that it appeared to me absurd.

Here is the description of the bedroom:

> . . . my walls were ornamented with curious objects, varying from caricatures and crucifixes to prints of prize-fights, fox-hunts, virgins, and Wagner. In one of the turrets I hung my clothes; in the other I put an altar on which I kept my books of prayer and a skull. . . . We

wore charming dressing-jackets, and sat up in bed with coloured cushions behind our backs, while the brothers and friends sat on the floor or in comfortable chairs round the room.

She says of herself elsewhere: "Bold as well as fearless, and always against convention, I was, no doubt, extremely difficult to bring up."   And in another place, making us wonder if she understands the meaning of the words, she writes: "Nevertheless we were all deeply religious, by which no one need infer that we were good."

The question is, not whether she was good, but whether she had the least notions of delicacy.

It is characteristic, I think, of Mrs. Asquith's mind that so much of the wit in her volume should be in the region of retort.   She is a past mistress in the art of the "back-answer," and seems to relish it in her friends. But reflection tells us that repartee is the language of self-assurance, its chief theatre the street corner. Experience shows, I think, that retort is seldom the utterance of a really beautiful and sensitive mind.

Here is a significant extract from her diary:

> Mamma is dead.   She died this morning, and Glen isn't my home any more.

The reader need not prepare himself for deep emotion. The diarist proceeds: "Mamma's life and death have taught me many things."   Then follows a long analysis

of the mother's character, whose body apparently was
not yet in its coffin.   For example:

> Few women have speculative minds, nor can they
> deliberate; they have instincts, quick apprehensions,
> and powers of observation. . . .   Mamma was in all
> these things like the rest of her sex.

I must confess that this shocks me.

I will give an incident which seems to me characteristic of a thoroughly degenerate age.

One night, as a young unmarried girl, Mrs. Asquith
went alone to the Opera House at Dresden.   She remembers what she wore on that occasion.   It was
something conspicuous—a scarlet dress, pearls, and a
black cloth cape.   She tells us that she was having "a
frank stare" round the house, when she caught sight of
an officer in a white uniform:

> He was a fine-looking young man, with tailor-made
> shoulders, a small waist, and silver and black on his
> sword-belt.   On closer inspection he was even hand-
> somer than I thought.

The white officer, we are told, began to look about
the house when his eyes caught Miss Tennant's red
dress.

> He put up his glasses and I instantly put mine down.
> Although the lights were lowered for the overture, I
> saw him looking at me for some time. . . .
> When the curtain dropped at the end of the first act,

I left the box. It did not take me long to identify the white officer. . . . As I passed him I had to stop for a moment for fear of treading on his outstretched toes. He pulled himself erect to get out of my way; I looked up and our eyes met; I don't think I blush easily, but something in his gaze may have made me blush. I lowered my eyelids and walked on.

It was raining that night and Miss Tennant could not get a cab, so she pulled her cloak over her head and started to walk home:

Suddenly I became aware that I was being followed; heard the even steps and the click of spurs of someone walking behind me; I should not have noticed this had I not halted under a lamp to pull on my hood, which the wind had blown off. . . . The street being deserted, I was unable to endure it any longer; I turned round and there was the officer. . . . He saluted me and asked me in a curious Belgian French if he might accompany me home. I said:

"Oh, certainly! But I am not at all nervous in the dark."

As they walked along together, this unknown officer and this future wife of a British Prime Minister, the following conversation occurred between them:

Officer: "You would not like to go and have supper with me in the private room of the hotel, no?"

Margot: "You are very kind, but I don't like supper; besides, it is too late." (Leaving his side to look at the number on the door.) "I am afraid we must part here."

Officer (drawing a long breath): "But you said I might accompany you to your home!"

Margot (with a slow smile): "I know I did; but this is my home."

He looked disappointed and surprised, but taking my hand he kissed it, then, stepping back, saluted, and said: "*Pardonnez-moi, mademoiselle.*"

So the incident ends, with an apology which appears to have ministered to Miss Tennant's pride. "*Pardonnez-moi, mademoiselle.*" He had mistaken her for—a lady who would go to supper with him. What a blunder!

But the incident is nothing. It is its publication that takes away the breath. Why is it published? What is the point of it? When you remember that Mrs. Asquith is fifty-six years of age, and reflected upon the fact that it served no political or social end to publish in 1920 so unpleasant an experience of her eventful past, you will agree that there is an element here of persisting indelicacy, which in a young woman would be disagreeable, but in an elderly woman is disgusting.

You see her nature when she tells you that she "listened closely" to Laura's warning about being "fast," deciding that the idea was absurd. She *thinks* where most people are guided by instinct. But even here she does not think very far. She did not think, for instance, in the matter of bedroom entertainments, whether it would be "absurd" for the maidservants in the attics to hold a bedroom salon—or should it be saloon?—with the knife-boy, the footmen, and the

© Paul Thompson

GENERAL SIR IAN HAMILTON

butler, while she and her sister entertained "company" on the floor below.   Apparently, however, she does not perceive that there is no logic in manners.   There is no reason in logic why she should not clean her teeth on the doorstep.   There is no reason in logic why she should not make a loud noise when she eats.   There is no reason in logic why she should not dig M. Bonvin in the ribs when she goes to luncheon at the Ritz.   Nice people do not do these things.   Neither do they ever ask themselves why they do not do them.   It is instinctive with them not to do such things.

Mrs. Asquith, however, is a law to herself.   That is why I call her a social anarchist.   That is why I say her influence has been ruinous.   But she has the wisdom of the serpent as well as its tongue.   She can be perfectly subdued on occasion.   She can be demure. Is she not devoted to Queen Alexandra?

She may be regarded, I think, as one of those electrical contrivances which can pass into the veins either a pleasant vibration, very beneficial to vitality, or a shock capable of destroying vitality altogether.   It is entirely a matter of the current.

She has no delicacy; she is proud of what she calls her "social courage," she is always against the conventions; but she has a certain amount of tact.   She would not switch on quite so much current for John Morley, or Gilbert Murray, as for lesser men, men of a more vigorous vitality.

4

This perhaps may explain the really beautiful and noble letters of Benjamin Jowett, which appear in this book, and even a letter quite astonishing and almost shocking which John Morley wrote to the lady at the time of her marriage.

John Morley has condemned fashionable society with a contempt as withering as Voltaire's, and with an austerity as high as Mill's. A score of fiery passages come into my mind. He speaks of fashionable life as "that dance of mimes," pours scorn on "that egoism which makes the passions of the individual his own law," and denounces the man of the world as "that worst enemy of the world." Who, in modern times, has lent to moral effort, to spiritual aspiration, a manlier hand than John Morley?

And yet, how does this great moralist, this burning reformer, this impassioned philosopher of history, write to a person so notorious for egoism and reckless self-assertion as Miss Margot Tennant?

He says: "*Don't improve by an atom.*"

I think John Morley's "don't improve" deserves to live in history.

In this letter he speaks of the people who wish Miss Margot Tennant to improve as "those impertinents," and says, "I very respectfully wish nothing of the sort." Note that "very respectfully."

Are the great so easily dazzled by a little boldness in the small? When we draw quite closely to them

are they great at all, these idols of our youth? I
wonder if indiscretion is not the greatest of all
iconoclasts.

Don't improve!—and society going down hill at that
time with both brakes off. Don't improve! —and
the other classes of the community looking to Fashion
as never before for its examples. Don't improve!—
and every philosopher of antiquity proclaiming that
goodness is something to be achieved by constant effort
and unwearying watchfulness. Don't improve!—and
he has applauded with all his eloquence the moral
earnestness of one who said "the greatest of all sins is
to be conscious of none."

It is kind to suppose that Mrs. Asquith tempers
the wind of her "social courage" to the shorn lamb
of philosophical innocence. The current changes with
the conditions. John Morley never felt, we may be
sure, that Miss Margot Tennant was a woman "whose
fire would blast the soul" of his friend, Henry Asquith;
and Peter Flower, we suspect, never dreamed of writing
a letter to this brilliant chameleon bidding her very
respectfully not to improve.

Mrs. Asquith, let me assure the reader, has many
gifts and graces to commend her. One of my greatest
friends is a friend of hers, and he tells me that he likes
her very much. Sir Arbuthnot Lane, no emotionalist,
has assured me of the same thing. Mrs. Drew, a first-
rate person, has written of her, if with some criticism,

yet also with evident affection.   Moreover, there are the letters of Jowett in this book to make one feel how easily Mrs. Asquith can control her current.

Mrs. Lloyd George once told me that no one could have been kinder to her when she first moved into Downing Street than Mrs. Asquith, who went out of her way to make the difficult path of Mrs. Lloyd George smooth and easy.   When Lord Harcourt's diaries are published people will understand what that kindness meant.   I know a few people who indeed speak warmly of her; but I know numbers of women who detest the very mention of her name.   They are not jealous.   They simply feel that her "social courage" is odious, a euphemism for effrontery.

Her attraction must have been far greater twenty or thirty years ago.   I think she dazzled people.   She was the herald of a new order; and even the great are not proof against a fresh sensation.   Stories floated through the world concerning "those extraordinary Tennant girls."   I remember a discussion at Ascot years ago concerning Margot Tennant, Henry James one of the listeners.   It was the old order holding up its hands in scandalised unbelief.   She may be called the Grandmother of the Flapper.

In the suburbs it was asked, is she the smart young lady of Mr. Hope's *Dolly Dialogues?*   and also, is she Mr. Benson's *Dodo?*   She was said to have dashed off the description of a certain great lady in these words:

"Rectitude, platitude, sailorhatitude." The good things not said by Lady Constance Hatch or Mrs. Willie James were credited to Mrs. Asquith. And all the bad things to be told about anyone were told about "Mrs. A."

She has now painted her own portrait, and scandal may take a long vacation. We know her, not only as she sees herself, but as she does not see herself, even in her own looking-glass.

There are certain things to like in her: her generosity, her kindness, her truthfulness (not her accuracy), and her freedom from snobbishness. But I miss in these pages, so full of aristocratic names and proud titles, to most of which are appended such phrases as "my friend," "my dear friend," "my dearest friend," "my beloved friend," the humble name of two people whose friendly kindness to her would seem to confer upon them at least a title to honourable mention. But likeable as certain people may find her, I have now no doubt, after reading her book, that I was right in the suggestion at which I permitted myself only to hint in *The Mirrors of Downing Street* concerning Mr. Asquith's fall from power. And I think I am right in saying now that her influence in English society has been corrupting and destructive. She seems to me definitely in arms against all those graces which are the very sinew of good manners.

Jowett, she says, was "apprehensive of my social reputation." And proceeds:

He was extremely simple-minded, and had a pathetic belief in the fine manners, high tone, wide education, and lofty example of the British aristocracy.   It shocked him that I did not share it: I felt his warnings much as a duck swimming might feel (*sic*) the cluckings of a hen on the bank

—a thing clearly impossible for anyone to achieve. But Mrs. Asquith seldom entered the diminishing circle where fine manners were to be found.   One is astonished in going through her pages to see how few people she knew intimately, whose influence one remembers with a still fragrant gratitude.   I do not think, for example, that she knew Lady Frederick Cavendish, or the beautiful Duchess of Westminster, or any of the Hamiltons, the Spencers, or the Howards. I do not think that she has been an intimate friend of the Portlands, or the Lansdownes, the Cecils, or the Percys.

When I was reading the chapters of her childhood, where she tells us that she loved climbing on the roof of the house, I wondered if it ever occurred to her that she might end in the basement.   A fall is so easy for heads not accustomed to great heights.   And when I came to the last page of this long pilgrimage through Vanity Fair which nevertheless leaves so much more to be said, I found the following passage:

An unfettered childhood and triumphant youth; a lot of love-making and a little abuse; a little fame and more abuse; a real man and great happiness; the love of children and seventh heaven; an early death and a *crowded memorial service.*

That final aspiration, which I have put into italics, seems to me to justify my speculation in the early pages regarding a fall to the basement, and also to justify my judgment that Mrs. Asquith's sensational career has not been good for the spiritual life of English society.

When she was a child and was brought down to the drawing-room, she would make entrance with the announcement, "Me's here!" That intense feeling of self-importance has remained with her to the end, and nothing that can be said of her book will shake the iron egoism of her character or make her feel for a moment that she has committed a grave indelicacy.

To the end she will live self-satisfied and flamboyant in an atmosphere of "caricatures and crucifixes"; she will assuredly have her desire in "a crowded memorial service," and I do not think it is unlikely that her first utterance in the next world will be, "Me's here!"

One of the chapters in *The Mirrors of Downing Street* which has been challenged by a somewhat intemperate criticism is that in which I hint as delicately as possible that Mrs. Asquith has not been a good influence on Mr. Asquith's career. Since those words were written, Mr. Wilfrid Scawen Blunt, a great friend of Mrs. Asquith, has published the second part of his *Diaries.*[1] In Octo-

[1] *My Diaries*, by Wilfrid Scawen Blunt.

ber, 1909, he had a conversation with Mr. Winston Churchill, who gave him the following information concerning Mr. Asquith:

"He will sit up playing bridge and drinking late at night. . . . Asquith has gone morally downhill.   From the Puritan he was, he has adopted the polite frivolities of society. . . .   He had gone all to pieces at one time, but pulled himself together when he became Prime Minister."

Mr. Dillon told the diarist the same thing in 1910: "He had been ruined by his second marriage to one who was a Tory at heart. . . .   Asquith was quite demoralised. . . .   Before his second marriage Asquith was quite different. . . .   He had no pretensions then to being anything but what he was, a Nonconformist of the middle-class; now he had adopted all the failings of the aristocracy."

Mr. Blunt says: "This evolution of the square-toed Asquith, with his middle-class Puritanical bringing up and his severity of conduct, into a 'gay dog' of London society is to me irresistibly funny."

It is that, too; but, in the first place, something much more serious.

CHAPTER V

A STUDY IN CONTRAST

Ah! if Madame de Stael had been Catholic, she would have been adorable, instead of famous.—JOSEPH DE MAISTRE.

The two images farthest removed from each other which can be comprehended under one term, are, I think, Isaiah, "Hear, O heavens, and give ear, O earth!"; and Levi, of Holywell Street, "Old Clothes!"; both of them Jews, you'll observe. Immane quantum discrepant!—S. T. COLERIDGE.

IT is the misfortune of many to suppose that every protest against badness is dictated by a partiality for gloom. Flippant people, with their tiresome *clichés*, their incessant giggling, and their little blasphemies, have not the least idea that the highest form of wit and the gayest exercise of good humour are to be found only among the noble-minded.

As a taste for loud music tends to degrade the ear till it is incapable not only of appreciating good music, but even of recognising it when it is heard, so the indulgence of the mind in feeble or second-rate humour leads at last to an incapacity for humour of the highest order. One seems to see in Fashion's appetite for the music of negro bands a return to the jungle, a return to a primitive state of society in which the buffon was held to be a humorist and the inventor of practical jokes was regarded as a master of wit.

I once asked a lady famous for her *mots* whether a certain royal personage who had often stayed in her houses was amusing in conversation. "Not in the least," she said. "When one said something *spirituel* he simply stared; at dinner he would often arrest the fork on its way to his mouth and inquire, What are they laughing at? But if on a shoot somebody caught his toe on a turnip and fell over, he would hold his side, shaking with laughter till the tears came."

Let me remind the age that Socrates was a playful spirit, that Erasmus was overflowing with good humour, that Dr. Johnson poured out capital jokes as copiously as tea, that few letters in the world compare with Edward FitzGerald's for wit, that Charles Lamb and Thomas Hood made as excellent puns as any of our day, that Lewis Carroll kindled the sweetest kind of laughter in the world's heart, that Calverley and Locker were charmingly amusing, and that no comic writer of our times has surpassed Charles Dickens for richness of humour or Thackeray for delicacy of wit.

All these men would not only have been displeased by the "social courage" of our contemporary Fashion, for each one of them was distinguished in one way or another for moral earnestness, but would have been

unable to see amusement in the things which now pass
for wit and humour.

Moreover, the bitterest and most consuming wit
of the eighteenth century, that of Voltaire in France
and Swift in England, had its rise, not in licence and
frivolity, but in moral rage and spiritual indignation.
Such wit might come again in this period, but not the
highest wit of all—the wit which has sweetness, radiance,
and warmth.

Fashion, then, in degrading manners and morals
has also degraded the happy playfulness of the human
spirit. This is matter for reflection. Life is no longer
amusing. It is not vivacious, but noisy. There is no
zest, no richness, no sparkle, no colour, no fire, no
splendour. It is drab. It is dreary. There are "crazes"
instead of stability. There is a rush for excitement, a
taste for cocktails and cocaine, a constant winding up of
the brain to experience reaction. The whole secret of
happiness, quietness at the centre, is lost. The one great
reward of existence, a sense of growth, is forgotten.

The truth is that licence always tends to produce an
intellectual marasmus; whereas obedience to law and
observance of rules string up the intellect to a condition
of the greatest health and activity. No form of wit is
more transient than the wit of the libertine. No wit is
so immortal as the wit of the moralist.

I will give a few examples of what Mrs. Asquith considers amusing:

. . . in a good-humoured way he made a butt of God.

Gladstone thinks my fitness to be Henry's wife ought to be prayed for like the clergy: Almighty and Everlasting God, Who alone workest great marvels.

"What is it that God has never seen, that kings see seldom, and that we see every day?"

Raymond instantly answered:

"A joke."

I felt that the real answer—which was "an equal" —was very tepid after this.

I heard her say to the late Lord Rothschild, one night at a dinner party: "And do you still believe the Messiah is coming, Lord Natty?"

These things appear in her book as witticisms. They are, apparently, the best that Fashion can give us. I suggest to the reader that he turn to the Letters of FitzGerald to see the wit that amused a less complex period and an altogether nobler mind. Or, let him read a chapter of Sir Thomas Browne, to see how loveliness of language goes with loveliness of mind.

One of the charges to be brought against Fashion, and it is by no means a light one, is the charge that it has depressed the human spirit and degraded the natural joy of the human heart.

As a contrast to Mrs. Asquith, let us consider the wife of another British Prime Minister, the wife of Gladstone. Here was one whose whole life was dominated by the highest conceivable sense of duty and who was profoundly religious. What did people say of her?

Her presence brought an atmosphere, a climate with it, all brightness, freshness, like sunshine and sea air.

You felt her splendid intuition, her swift motions, the magic of her elusive phrases, her rapid courage, her never-failing fund of sympathy, her radiance, her gaiety of heart, her tenderness of response.

Her discretion as to public secrets, *of which she knew all*, was really extraordinary; she was willing, if necessary, to allow herself in conversation to appear almost a fool, in order to conceal the fact of her knowledge.

She radiated tenderness.

Religion, not forced, not obtruded, but as natural and vital as fresh air was, not an adjunct of life, but life itself.

She had a heavenly sense of fun, but its manner of expression was all her own.   There was nothing on earth to compare to the twinkle in her eye.

In her admirable memoir of her mother, which is, I think, an authentic portrait of a Victorian lady, Mrs. Drew gives some examples of Catherine Gladstone's fun:

Of a good-hearted bustling lady she would say, "In she walked with her *Here I am* hat."

Asked to describe a lady's dress . . . after picturing the general effect, she paused: "As to the body—well—I can only describe it as a *Look at Me* body!"

On another occasion she was speaking about the un-loverlike relations of a newly engaged couple: "To be sure," she said, "they did sit side by side upon the couch; but they looked just like a coachman and footman on the box, so stiff and upright, you could always see the light between."[1]

[1] *Catherine Gladstone*, by Mary Drew.   This book, which presents us with a most beautiful picture of William and Catherine Gladstone's life,

With a vivacity and a joyousness which would have captivated such spirits as Edward FitzGerald, Charles Kingsley, or Thackeray, Catherine Gladstone possessed a profound depth of inward seriousness which was like the presence of an angel.

It is only when one comes to read Mrs. Drew's monograph that one realises what the nation lost in Gladstone, and how politics have rushed downhill since his day.

One night as he walked through the London streets with a friend, Gladstone turned back to speak to a prostitute, and presently rejoined his friend with the woman at his side.   The friend whispered, "But what will Mrs. Gladstone say if you take this woman home?"   He answered, "It is to Mrs. Gladstone I am taking her."

Few people know that Gladstone gave himself with the deepest passion and the highest consecration to the bitter work of rescuing degraded women.   This noble passion, which I have reason to know began while he was at Oxford, lasted to the end of his life.   The dangers of such work had no terrors for him.   Extraordinary gossip floated through the haunts of scandal.   Among the base it was whispered, "The heel of Achilles!" Some of his friends would have dissuaded him from labours which almost invited the political spy and the social slanderer to destroy his reputation.   But Glad-

---

is essential, as a well-known statesman has written an understanding of Lord Morley's voluminous *Life*.

stone could not be turned.   Every woman saved by his efforts, every woman restored to womanhood, every woman created anew in faith and purity was a fresh incentive to his zeal.   And in this work, as in everything else, Catherine Gladstone was his partner.   Mrs. Gladstone and her friend Lady Lothian (this fact, I believe, has never been mentioned till now) went out regularly at night in places like Leicester Square, Coventry Street, and the Haymarket, seeking young girls and carrying them off to homes of rescue.

The story of this difficult and heroic work of William and Catherine Gladstone has not yet been told to the world, and I can only hint at it here.   It is one of the most romantic, as it is one of the most moving, stories in human biography.   The documents, I believe, are as numerous as the political documents; they witness to the fact that the Gladstones were not content to save girls from brothels and the streets, but that they followed their history from Clewer[1] into the world, and never ceased to feel a poignant personal interest in the moral and spiritual progress of the very least of those they saved.   When time permits this story of the Gladstones to be told to the world, I believe it will give mankind a new enthusiasm for the pressing work of

---

[1] This great House of Mercy, near Windsor, embraces an orphanage a penitentiary, and a beautiful chapel.   The Gladstones planned and shared with Mr. Monsell in its establishment.

saving the womanhood of a Christian nation from an Asiatic pollution.

Here is one incident to show the dangers that they ran:

Sir Howard Vincent, Chief of the Police, consulted Mr. George Russell on a grave difficulty. Mr. Gladstone, he said, was followed on all his walks at night by detectives of the highest character, men whom he trusted firmly; this on account of the Irish troubles. But even the most trusted of men might fall a victim on some occasion to the offer of a dazzling bribe. Such a bribe was now being offered; one of the most powerful and highly placed men in the opposing party was offering a large sum of money for evidence convicting Mr. Gladstone of entering a house of ill-fame. In these circumstances, he felt strongly that Mr. Gladstone should be warned of the danger.

It is interesting to reflect that while Gladstone was heroically struggling with ignorance and prejudice to settle the Irish Question before it became a revolutionary question, here was a chief member of the party which opposed him seeking to prevent that merciful act of statesmanship by striking at Gladstone's moral character in the spirit of an assassin.

Mr. Russell shrank from confronting Gladstone with this horrible news. He suggested to Sir Howard Vincent that he should consult Mr. Gladstone's secretary, Sir Edward Hamilton. Sir Edward Hamilton

RT. HON. ARTHUR JAMES BALFOUR

saw the peril, but not without some fear and trembling agreed to warn the Prime Minister.

Gladstone was seated at his table, writing. He looked up as the secretary entered, his pen still resting on the paper.

"What is it?"

He did not like being disturbed.

The secretary, making an effort, told the news.

Gladstone never changed his position. His face hardened a little, that was all. Then, in his deep, baying voice, he said very slowly to the young man:

"This is a subject on which it has been my invariable rule to keep silence." A pause. "But do you suppose I did not count the cost, every cost, when first I set my hand to this work? And do you imagine that at my advanced age, and with the accumulated experience of my life, my work or actions are at this stage undertaken in any haphazard manner, without full and grave consideration? I thank you for your warning. I recognise what it must have cost you to come before me with such a message. It must have cost you a great deal. I thank you for it."

A slight movement of his head dismissed the secretary and Gladstone continued his writing. And he continued his work of rescue to his life's end.

I told this story to one of the greatest men of our time, whose whole life has been inspired by a deep admiration for Gladstone's moral idealism. "Why

5

can't this story be told?" he demanded.   I explained
that there still existed people who would like to believe
evil of Gladstone, low-minded people who would not
scruple to whisper that in secret he was a vicious man.
My friend thought for a moment.   Then he said:
"How old was Gladstone when he died?   Over eighty.
Was his face the face of a sensualist?   Do people think
that a man could live to that age with a secret vice, and
show no sign of it in his face?   You tell me this idea
began with him at Oxford.   Why, at forty his face
would have betrayed him to all the world, if he had had
such a weakness in his heart.   But look at his face all
through his life!   Look at it when he was eighty!   I
don't think you could say it was the face of a satyr.
Why, it was like an eagle's!"

Gladstone felt that this work was too sacred and too
dreadful for conversation.   He never referred to it in
public.   Even his most intimate friends were not aware
of it.   Because of his extreme delicacy in the matter,
there were those who believed evil of him.   He knew it.
It made no difference to him.   Not a day passed in that
long, stormy, and most busy life which was untouched,
if even by a mere record in a book or a letter to Clewer,
by this passion of his consecrated soul.

One of Gladstone's friends, a distinguished and now
venerable lady, tells me the following story, related to
her by Sir Henry James, afterwards Lord James of
Hereford:

On one occasion, when Mr. Gladstone was returning from the House of Commons on a miserable wet night in November, he saw an unfortunate woman crouching upon the steps of the Duke of York's monument. He stopped and spoke to her, and asked her why she did not go home. She replied, she had none. He bade her rise and follow him the short way that led to Carlton Gardens, where he was then living. He was alone in London, his family at Hawarden. He let himself into the house with his latch-key, and found his frugal supper prepared in his library. Adjoining this was the room he used when alone in London. He gave the woman, cold and drenched as she was, some food; he then sent her into the adjoining room, bade her undress, dry her clothes at the fire kept burning for him, and try to rest. Meanwhile he locked the door of communication between them, sat up all night, reading and writing, and when the morning dawned, let the woman go forth warm and comfortable, with a few coins for her breakfast, and probably some good advice and further instructions.

Such was the man who was helped at every point of his life by Catherine Gladstone, and not least of all in this deep passion for saving the fallen. Of them both, when he lay dying, the wife of Archbishop Benson wrote:

Their kindness and thought and tenderness are indescribable. I saw her again yesterday, and thanked her as well as I could. They tell me that what helps him most is anything that is said of his in any way *helping the world.*

Here is a picture of them at the end of their days:

It was the habit of their lives to go every day to church before breakfast. They enjoyed the walk, nearly a mile uphill, in the early freshness of the morning, and winter or summer, storm or sunshine, saw them going to worship in Hawarden Church, Mrs. Gladstone scattering the path with the letters which she read on the way. Not even the early cups of tea, indispensable to most people, broke their fast.

At the age of eighty-three or eighty-four he said: "I am afraid I must ask you to keep Petz (a favourite dog) from coming to church with me. You see, I have to throw sticks for him to pick up, and stooping every other minute to get one and then throw it is too hard work on the hill."

"They were moved," we read, "by the same ardour to gather the very best, the richest out of life. To them life was not a thing to be idled and pleasured away; it was a sacred trust that implied true and laudable service to God and man. *They lifted it to a new level.*"

The record of these two lives is as fresh and beautiful as a bright morning in April. Their friends were not less brilliant, and not less exalted, than those whose names appear in contemporary memoirs; they themselves were neither heavy nor dull; the temptations of the world surrounding them on every side were as great as any that now destroy the joy and beauty of human society; but there was this vital difference between them and us, between then and now—the centre of life for people like the Gladstones was moral earnestness.

That was their *strength*. They knew, as Joseph de Maistre said, that constraint does not weaken, but strengthens. Their wit was brighter because blasphemy was forbidden, and dirtiness was impossible. Their playfulness was keener because their work was serious. There was no sprawling of their minds in one direction or another because restraint was as natural to them as honesty. There were boundaries, there were laws, there was a sense of decency. Manners were an expression of morality.

I do not know of any more striking contrast to the personality of Mrs. Asquith than the personality of Catherine Gladstone. It is striking because the similarities are so numerous. They not only filled precisely the same place in our national and social life, but at many points their natures, their temperaments, were identical. Mrs. Gladstone was all rush and vivacity. She hated routine. She loved adventure. She was sudden and unexpected. She overflowed with good nature. She sparkled with vivacity. She loved life, loved power, and loved crowds of people. It was she, not Gladstone, who hated the idea of resignation. It was she who was "ever a fighter." It was she who wanted the battle and the victory. Like Mrs. Asquith, too, she was wearied by bores and paid no attention to the details of etiquette, the mere forms of convention. She had "nature." She had "social courage." She "let herself go," says Father Waggett, but adds, "It was a charming creature to let go."

In her life, too, as in Mrs. Asquith's, there was a time when Fashionable Society was bitterly opposed to all she stood for in politics, and a time when a Radical colleague of her husband deserted the standard to strike the blow that meant defeat.

But how different the two women—these two women who were so like at a score of points!

Mrs. Gladstone could not have hung a caricature in the vicinity of a crucifix. She could not have seen amusement in wit that "made a butt of God." She could not have published to the world a narration of her love-affairs and her confinements. Why?

Something restrained her audacity, something repressed the ebullience of her high spirits, something controlled her impetuous spontaneity.

At the centre of her life, deep below the flashing surface of her social existence, was a profound reverence for the spiritual truth of humanity, a piercing sense of the reality of the Infinite, a pervasive humility of soul. And so, unlike Mrs. Asquith, who *thought* and *decided* in the matter of bedroom receptions, it is written of Catherine Gladstone, "Her trust in the guidance of instinct and impulse was absolute. Already, while others argued the way, she had reached the goal."

It was with her as it was with Goethe, and as it has never been with Mrs. Asquith; an *inward earnestness* saved her from all vulgarities, and made her noble, beautifully noble, in spite of all her eccentricities.

The youth of Goethe was filled with a thousand trivialities—German trivialities, sentimental, romantic, and tailor-made trivialities.   One reads that record not merely with impatience, but sometimes even with disgust.   He is not only a foppish philanderer and an intellectual prig; he is utterly insincere, utterly wanting in the virtues of the gentleman.

He himself came to wonder how his character emerged from that period, and how his genius survived it.   This pigmy, how did he become a giant?—this ephemeron, how did he become immortal?   "Of all the sons of genius," says Hume Brown, "none has been freer than Goethe was in his maturer years from every form of vanity and self-consciousness."   How did this come to pass?   In his youth he might have been one of the figures in such a book as Mrs. Asquith's biography; in his maturity he could not have read such a book without nausea.   By what power was such a miracle worked?

Goethe himself tells us that it was "an inward earnestness."   At the circumference of his soul was frivolity, sentimentalism, insincerity; but at the centre, waiting to save him when he would be still, was this inward earnestness, this "instinct for self-mastery," this feeling that life was a great thing, a high thing, a deep thing, a divine mystery, and that the work of life was to perfect the soul.

It is for lack of this one thing, *inward earnestness*,

this one thing which saved Goethe, this one thing that made Catherine Gladstone a different person from Margot Asquith, that society is now drifting so far out of its course.

CHAPTER VI

ILL EFFECTS

It is something to have an influence on the fortunes of mankind; it is greatly more to have an influence on their intellects. —W. S. LANDOR.

You pass by a little child, you pass by, spiteful, with ugly words, with wrathful heart; you may not have noticed the child, but he has seen you, and your image, unseemly and ignoble, may remain in his defenceless heart. You don't know it, but you may have sown an evil seed in him and it may grow.— DOSTOEVSKY.

For by a word we wound a thousand.—SIR THOMAS BROWNE.

LEST a too indulgent, perhaps I may be allowed to say a too shallow, reader should think I magnify the importance of people like Mrs. Asquith and Colonel Repington, holding it better to ignore them than further to advertise their existence by reprobation however just, I will here endeavour to show how far the influence of such characters may carry, to the detriment of England and the progress of civilisation.

Both these books, the *Autobiography* and the *Diaries*,

have been well published. Their sales have been prodi-
gious. Here in the British Islands they have had
thousands of readers, and in America and the Dominions
the numbers must be calculated by scores of thousands.
Both books, in two different ways, appeal to an almost
universal curiosity; the one promises insight into the
social mysteries of English aristocracy, the other insight,
into the political mysteries of allied statesmanship
during the crisis of the World War. Colonel Repington's social gossip, it must be understood, is only a
comic chorus to genuine information and excellent
criticism concerning a vast tragedy. His book is a work,
I imagine, which no serious student of the War can
afford to overlook. For myself, knowing something of
that inner history, I willingly confess that I read these
two volumes with an unflagging interest.

The appeal, then, of both books is not to be exag-
gerated. It is natural that they should be read far and
wide. They are genuine histories. In America, where
those of us who seek the world's peace must desire men
and women to think well of us, and in our Dominions,
where respect and affection for English traditions is the
very centre of that spontaneous loyalty which holds the
Commonwealth together, these books have carried a
very important message from England—a message
which cannot be ignored or suppressed, a message
which has penetrated deeply, a message which is not
likely to be forgotten in our generation, and the con-

sequences of which may go on for a period which no man can measure.

I would ask the reader to see that there are two ways in which these books are acting on the minds of men and women all over the world.

First of all, there is the obvious effect on people of intelligence—contempt of English aristocracy and contempt of English politics. Second, there is the effect on people of inferior intelligence—imitation of our worst qualities.

Both of these effects are bad. We must deplore the fact that because of these two books thousands of intelligent people all over the world are thinking of us with contempt; and equally we must deplore the fact that because of these two books thousands of unintelligent people are confirmed in flippancy, cynicism, vulgarity, and braggart ostentation.

As an example of the first effect, I will quote a passage from a review of Mrs. Asquith's book which appeared in *The New Republic* of America.

After a scornful examination of the autobiography, holding the writer up to the ridicule of all his educated readers, the critic pauses at the end of his analysis to make this remark:

And yet I subscribe myself a grateful reader of Mrs. Asquith's autobiography. I had a few lingering doubts as to the great social tradition of English politics, the Saturday-to-Monday refreshment of tired statesmen by untiring hostesses, the comradeship of aristocrats and political thinkers and souls. But this lengthy public dilatation of Mrs. Asquith's heart has settled for me the old notion that woman ever could have, much less ever had, a suitable place behind the throne. Behind the throne of man, as Mrs. Asquith exhibits it, there may always be a place for women of the pillowing variety, women who really like to stand waiting with the sponge and the smelling-salts and the towels. But for an aggressive personality like Mrs. Asquith, genuine child of "a man whose vitality, irritability, energy, and impressionability amounted to genius," this false rôle of subordination has turned her from a beaver into something smaller and less pleasant, and exposed her to the perceptive as a pest. Had she been an educated woman, and disciplined, and yet subordinate, could she have turned her life to advantage? I suppose so, as any man might. But being a woman born into a society where her game was to be charming, and where she had no chance to be seriously educated, we find her at the age of fifty-six publishing idiocies that Marie Bashkirtseff was too sophisticated to utter at fourteen, and never once attaining Marie Bashkirtseff's noble realisation that "if this book is not the *exact*, the *absolute*, the *strict* truth, it has no *raison d'être*."

These idiocies and, one must say, vulgarities, are not of themselves important. What does it matter how much this woman tells the gaping public about her flirtations, her self-estimates, her husband's prayers, and her confinements? The thing that matters is to see a fund of human nature squandered in horrible heedlessness on the enormous trivialities of the privileged class.

From this perfectly just and contemptuous criticism we must infer that there are numbers of educated

Americans whose affection for England has been weakened, and who have perhaps ceased to believe that the privileged classes in England have any contribution to make to the higher life of the human race. Such an effect I regard as deplorable; coming, as it does, at a particularly critical juncture of inter-state politics, I do not think I exaggerate in saying that this effect is disastrous. For is it altogether unreasonable to suppose that if there existed at this time a deep affection and a profound confidence between the Republic of the United States and the British Commonwealth such a great step might be taken towards disarmament as might lead in a generation to the peace of the world?

I propose in the next chapters to show that both Mrs. Asquith and Colonel Repington convey a false impression of English society, to show, at any rate, that there are people of the privileged classes in these islands mindful of their great responsibilities, whose lives are beautiful, unselfish, useful—people who still quietly maintain beyond the reach of the public limelight those noble traditions of the human soul which have distinguished the English Gentry at almost every period of our history. I hope, that is to say, that I may be able to achieve at least something in the direction of mitigating among thoughtful people here in Great Britain, and in the Dominions, and in the United States, the unfortunate impression conveyed by Mrs. Asquith and Colonel Repington.

Before proceeding to that pleasant work, I would remind the reader once again of the great importance of apparently trivial things.

Let him pause for a moment to consider the case of Russia. For a hundred years we have thought of Russia as a vast military power, or an empire groaning under the tyranny of an autocrat, or a country in which literature and art were manifesting themselves in new and brilliant forms, or as a nation seething with political ideas of a wild and revolutionary character.

These matters were great enough, obvious enough, for our observation and our interest. We should have regarded a man as tiresome who told us that the one thing in Russia worthy of our attention was the lack of moral earnestness in all classes of that human chaos. But this fact, nevertheless, was the greatest thing in Russia; everything else in that huge empire was in sober truth but as so much spindrift to this deep groundswell of the Russian tragedy. There was one who saw the truth, one who perceived "the littleness in which the greatness of human life is hidden," one who prophesied years ago the universal calamity which has plunged his country into abject misery, and is still hanging like a tempest over the uneasy peace of Versailles; but because he did not come before us as a Nihilist, or a strident philosopher of Bolshevism, because he had nothing to say about the great rivers of Damascus, and insisted only on the need of Jordan, because, that is, he was nothing picturesque and striking and new, only a moralist, a moralist insisting on the vexatious necessity for truth in the inward parts—what a provincialism!—what a platitude!—we ignored his message and missed the secret of Russia's woe.

This man, Fyodor Dostoevsky, makes one of the characters in *The Possessed* speak as follows:

> . . . crime is no longer insanity, but simply common sense, almost a duty; anyway, a gallant protest.
>
> The Russian God has already been vanquished by cheap vodka. The peasants are drunk, the mothers are drunk, the children are drunk, the churches are empty. . . .
>
> Oh, this generation has only to grow up.
>
> Ah, what a pity there's no proletariat! But there will be, there will be, we are going that way.
>
> . . . One or two generations of vice are essential now; monstrous, abject vice by which a man is transformed into a loathsome, cruel, egoistic reptile.
>
> We will proclaim destruction . . . we'll set fires going. We'll set legends going. Every scurvy "group" will be of use. . . . There will be an upheaval. There's going to be such an upset as the world has never seen before. . . . Russia will be overwhelmed with darkness, the earth will weep for its old gods.

The important thing in Russia was not the political government, but the common everyday fact that the peasants were drunk, that the mothers were drunk, that the children were drunk, and that the priests, with their mistresses and their illegitimate children, were drunk too.

"Listen," cries Dostoevsky's character, announcing a truth of the highest importance. "I've seen a child of six years old leading home his drunken mother, whilst she swore at him with foul words."

Which was the greater peril of Russia in those days, despotism or immorality, an absolutist Tsar or a drunken mother?

There is a despotism in Russia at the present time. One of the hungry citizens of Moscow, pointing to the Kremlin, said to Mr. Bertrand Russell, "In there they have enough to eat." Always there must be a privileged class, always there must be masters. Revolution can do nothing but displace one authority by another. The character of civilisation depends absolutely on the moral character of that authority, whatever it calls itself, and that moral character will always chiefly be determined by the moral character of the mass.

Do we realise that the "world tragedy" of Russia is mainly the tragedy of two cities? The millions of peasants are neither hungry nor cold. The change of government has meant little to them; their lives are not altered, nor their fortunes. The crushing tragedy is felt mainly in the two principal cities of that vast empire, Moscow and Petrograd, where people are not only hungry and cold, but intimidated by a worse form of slavery than ever existed under the Tsars.

How is this possible? How are a few fanatical followers of Karl Marx able to hold millions of people in

THE RT. HON. W. E. GLADSTONE

1858

From a portrait by Watts in the National Portrait Gallery

the iron grip of a despotism which crushes both soul and body?

The answer is that the multitudes composing the Russian Empire long ago have ceased to feel the infinite importance of moral ideas. Because there was no cleavage in their minds between right and wrong there is now no vigorous public opinion, no moral force against which tyranny of any kind would oppose itself in vain. Russia has a thousand qualities which deserve the admiration of mankind, but lacking this one quality of moral earnestness it is stricken with death.

Of all intellectual shallowness none is more disastrous to the higher life of the human race than that which ignores the attitude of average men and women to the simplest questions of right and wrong.

"Steadily, silently, the inevitable process of change goes on, and neither the individual himself nor any of those nearest to him may notice how, in the one case, his character is being strengthened and elevated, and, in the other case, is being weakened and lowered."

6

CHAPTER VII

THE OTHER SIDE

*Everyone carries with him a certain moral atmosphere,
which to a great extent determines the relations into which he
comes with his fellow men. . . . Thus men are continually
shedding off, as it were, some part of their personality into
the society around them. And the tone of this society is the
result, not so much of the deliberate attempt of the members of
it to influence each other, as of the unconscious action and
reaction of their characters . . . the whole weight of the evil
that is in our society is dragging us down, and the whole force
of the good that is in it is helping us up.*—EDWARD CAIRD.

*Moral principles rarely act powerfully upon the world,
except by way of example or ideals.*—LECKY.

IT is one of their many deplorable consequences that
the books of Mrs. Asquith and Colonel Repington, while
perfectly true of the sets in which their writers move,
quite cruelly misrepresent English society as a whole.

You may easily see how false is the impression these
books convey if you recall for a moment the immense
volume of devoted service rendered by people of leisure
during the War. A foreign reader might well conclude
from Colonel Repington's book that England took that

great struggle with fun and frolic, and that her one anxiety, while enjoying a "good time," or as good a time as the circumstances permitted, was to defeat Germany in the field.

There was another anxiety. Never before in the history of England did so deep and earnest a desire to minister to the soul of humanity move upon the waters of our national life. Never before were all classes of the community in closer touch. And this great labour, so far as aristocracy is concerned, was done, not by fashionable people who hurried to the photographer in their nurse's dress or their Red Cross uniform, not by people who discovered in the War an opportunity to display their talents as actors and actresses, but by people who were doing solid work before the War, and who are still quietly toiling for the higher life of the human race.

It may help to mitigate some of the worst consequences of Colonel Repington's book if I set down here a few memories of London during the War; a few memories of people in my own acquaintance who took part in that vast labour of humanitarianism which transfigured the national life at a period of enormous stress and almost unimaginable sorrow.

I recall a conversation with Mr. J. R. Clynes in the year 1917. He spoke hopefully of the end of the War, and hopefully of the reconstruction period which would succeed our military activity. He based his optimism

solely on the good understanding which had then come
to exist between the various classes of the community.
The War, he said, had introduced the classes into a
domestic intimacy which was making for an affectionate
understanding of their difficulties.

This unity of spirit seemed to him so wonderful a
thing that he refused to believe the nation would ever
again revert to the crudities of class hatred. We are
already in some danger of losing this great gain.

Little, I think, is known to the public of the work
done by a body of English ladies to convince the
soldiers of our Dominions that England cared for them
and was profoundly mindful of their self-sacrifice. This
work is eminently suitable for mention in the present
place, since it took the admirable form of introducing
the soldiers of our Dominions into the best home-life
of England—a home-life which some people might say
had ceased to exist. Its form was purely domestic. It
was as intimate as hospitality of that nature could
possibly be. Because of this domestic and intimate
character, it did more for England, I think, at any rate
more for the great moral principles of the British Commonwealth, than any other philanthropic work of a
patriotic nature.

It is impossible for me to mention the names of all
those ladies who rendered this immeasurable service
to the good name of England; the reader must kindly
bear in mind that I set down here only the names of

those few who are either known to me personally, or whose extraordinary influence came to my knowledge from actual experience. There was a great body of people whose excellent work did not come within the narrow range of my own small life, and whose services may well have been as great, or greater, than those to which, for the purpose of my requirements, I shall now refer. These good and noble women will not resent the omission of their names from my pages; the gratitude of men and women in all parts of the British Empire is their ample reward. I am more likely to offend those ladies of my acquaintance whose names do appear in these pages, since, even for a good purpose, they dislike any public mention of their work. But this risk I am content to run, in order to convince as wide a public as I can reach, both here and across the seas, that aristocracy in England has not gone over bag and baggage to the enemy of Christian civilisation.

In order that the officers from our Dominions should not feel themselves strangers and aliens at the heart of the Empire, a number of ladies organised a system of hospitality which aimed to be as free from the spirit of institutionalism as loving service and a deep concern for the good name of England could make it. The officers were to be sought out in camps, barracks, clubs, hostels, hospitals, and convalescent homes. They were to be invited to visit certain of the best houses in London. Their hostesses were to entertain them just as they entertained their own friends. And those officers who expressed a desire to see something of English country life were to be the guests of ladies in all parts of the United Kingdom. In short, officers from our Dominions arriving in England were to be treated like the friends and relations of the very best families in England.

I will mention the names of a few ladies who took part in this work merely to convince the reader that the names in Colonel Repington's book do not by any means exhaust the peerage. But when I say that in Lady Harrowby's organisation alone there were 695 hostesses who entertained these officers, the reader will see how impossible it is for me to mention more than a very few names.

But here are these few names: The Duchess of Argyll, the Duchess of Atholl, the Duchess of Norfolk, the Duchess of Wellington, the Marchioness of Winchester, the Marchioness of Salisbury, the Countess of Harrowby, the Countess of Hardwicke, the Countess of Strathmore, the Countess of Cromer, the Countess of Derby, the Countess of Glasgow, the Countess of Yarborough, the Countess Fortescue, the Countess of Dunmore, the Dowager Countess of Jersey, the Dowager Countess of Clanwilliam, Lady Hambleden, Lady Ampthill, Lady Northcote, Lady Carmichael, Lady Zouche, Lady Portman, Lady Farnham, Lady Harcourt, Lady Gladstone, Lady de l'Isle and Dudley, Lady Dunleath, Lady Hilda Murray, Lady Howard de Walden, Lady Doreen Long, Lady Frances Ryder (a great driving force in more than one organisation), Lady Mary Morrison, Lady Alice Fergusson, Lady Mabel Kenyon Slaney, Lady Angela Campbell, the Hon. Mrs. Henry Edwardes, the Hon. Mrs. Hope Morley, the Hon. Margaret Colville (who also worked unsparingly to trace missing officers), the Hon. Harriet Phipps, Mrs. Cuninghame of Craigends, Miss Macdonald of the Isles, Mrs. Abel Smith, of Cole Orton, Miss Agnes Bowen, daughter of a late Governor of Queensland, and the two daughters of Sir Arthur Lawley.

It would only bother the reader to give the statistics of the various organisations with which these ladies worked, but when I say that one of them alone was responsible for hospitality to 100,000 officers, something of the magnitude of the work will be understood. I prefer to give a few slight sketches of these hostesses, in order that the reader may understand the character of the hospitality extended to our Dominion soldiers. It was the *nature* of this hospitality which made it different from almost every other form of war work, and it is by understanding its nature or character that the reader will best enter into a truer knowledge of English social life.

Lady Harrowby, who with her daughter, Lady Frances Ryder, and a staff of ladies, did a vast work of organisation, besides acting as hostess in many entertainments, tells me that, looking back over the period

of the War, she is inclined to envy Mrs. Henry
Edwardes more than anybody else who took part in
offering hospitality to our Dominion soldiers. The
reason for this noble envy will declare itself in the
narrative which follows.

This Mrs. Edwardes is pinned to her chair by rheu-
matoid arthritis as effectually as Prometheus to his rock.
She can lift her hands a few inches, and that is all. In
everything else she is helpless. Never once before the
War did I hear her utter a single complaint, and since
the War she is even inclined to bless her illness, for by
its very nature it enabled her to enter into the closest
possible intimacy with her visitors. She could do nothing to amuse them; she could do everything to know
them. Unable to attend meetings or to take part in the
mechanism of organisation, this charming woman, who
has known courts and capitals, and who is so well read
and so spiritually wise, remained in her chair, and round
that chair in her drawing-room gathered officers from
every quarter of the British Commonwealth, telling her
about their homes, and listening to her good counsel
with reverence and affection.

That chair in the drawing-room of Herbert Crescent
became for me a veritable throne of England, and the
stooping lady, clothed in beautiful white draperies and
old lace, who sat there surrounded by soldiers from
beyond the seas, seemed to me a reincarnation of the
Victorian spirit of domestic life.

Her graciousness, her exceeding gentleness, her perfect sympathy with human nature, are all strung together by a vigorous intellectual good sense which gives power to her sweetness.   No woman could be more tender, none more free from sentimentalism. She is wise, but she is infinitely sweet.   A profound and beautiful spiritual life is the secret of her attractive power.

The reader will perceive that I do not exaggerate the national and imperial influence of this good woman, whose name finds no mention in the pages of Mrs. Asquith and Colonel Repington; if he will kindly glance over the following quotations which I make at random from the thousands of letters written by Dominion soldiers, and also by their mothers in distant lands, which Mrs. Edwardes received during the War, and is receiving to this day.

One officer writes of a most gallant dead comrade:

Among the papers he carried was a request that should he be killed in action he would like one of his friends to write and let you know. . . .   He told me once that his chief pride in winning his decorations was that you would know he had tried to make good.

An Australian mother who had visited England wrote to Mrs. Edwardes, saying:

Because I was a stranger and you made me feel so much at home and so very happy with you, I have tried to make the girls who are so bravely coming 12,000 miles to marry our Australian soldiers feel that in me they have a real friend; so you see how far your influence has reached.

No wonder that a South African soldier should write to this noble lady in the following words:

> I leave England to-day with a heart overflowing with gratitude to and affection for my mother country. . . . You have done more to bind the Empire together by your kindness and sympathy and friendship . . . than statesmanship can ever hope to achieve.

From the mother of a fallen Canadian came this letter:

> I hope these few flowers will convey to you a little of the gratitude I find so hard to express, for all your loving sympathy and kindness to me.   All my life your goodness will remain as one of the brightest memories in my darkest hour.
>
> It is not given to every woman to have had such perfect love, friendship, and understanding as my son gave me, and although my pride in the knowledge of his having done his duty so nobly is great, there are hours when the thought that I shall never see him again is almost more than I can bear.

You may see what she was to these superb soldiers and their mothers, and what her gentleness meant to the Empire, when you know that an Australian could write to her from the trenches as "My dear English Mother." A Canadian exclaims in a letter after an action, "How deeply I feel towards you and other splendid women of your class in England!" A South African mother writes thanking her for kindness to her son, and for her kindness to "all other Colonials who perhaps have no mother to write for them."

What a wonderful work for England! How silent, how unknown! Picture to yourself the London of those years—the feasting at restaurants, the roaring music-halls, the rackety night-clubs, the jests and anecdotes at such dinner-tables as Colonel Repington frequented as a relief to his work; picture the streets as we knew them in those days—the procession of motor-cars, the parade of fashionable people, the crowds of prostitutes, the rush of newsboys, the glitter of shop windows, the flags flying from the house-tops, the sense everywhere of a carnival in mid-Lent, of a brass band in Gethsemane; all this in the public streets, and here in a little house in Knightsbridge, men from every part of England's vast Empire gathered round the chair of a frail and suffering woman, one of the few remaining friends of Queen Victoria, telling her of their homes across the seas, their mothers, their sisters, and finding in her words a music that was like the sound of a mother's voice.

Many of those gallant men, suddenly ordered back to the carnage of the trenches, calling in Herbert Crescent to say good-bye to the woman who had meant so much to them, and finding that she had been carried up to her bed, would ask whether they might not be allowed to see her, if only for a moment.   They wanted her to be their last memory of England.

In this way it happened that many an Anzac, Canadian, and South African was conducted to the invalid's bedroom and received her blessing kneeling at her bedside.   The reverence they felt for her was unbounded; their love for her was a part of their love for England. "You have made so many of us feel," wrote one, "that England really does *care*."

What strikes me so much in these letters from the battlefields is their cheerfulness.   Men wrote to her from the front trenches, in conditions of inexpressible horror, wishing her "A Merry Christmas," inquiring after her health, and describing a battle in the terms of the football field.   "I am always afraid of being a nuisance," writes one young officer, in a preface to his spirited account of a great fight.   "I am feeling fine," says another, after a terrible battle, "this life agrees with me."   And another, after recounting the tale of a German attack, assures her that "life here is very comfortable."   They wanted to cheer her up.   In none of these thousands of letters have I come across a single whine, the smallest grouse, the least cry for sympathy. The most that a young Canadian will say after a terrible battle at night is the comment, "He is a fool who says there is no God!"

I think those men must have realised how deeply, how truly, she felt for them, when her letters reached them in France—dictated letters, but almost always with a few last words written by her own poor tortured hand; the hand that was once so beautiful, the hand which sculptors copied in Rome—a few words of blessing and affection. "How can I thank you sufficiently," writes a South African, "for the dear little diary you sent me as a keepsake. I will carry it with me always while campaigning."

Think of those little gifts crossing the seas from this London drawing-room to soldiers of the Empire fighting in every quarter of the globe! One is so tempted to forget that the night-club was not the only form of hospitality which London offered to the sons of the British Commonwealth.

To this day Mrs. Edwardes is receiving letters from all parts of the Empire. For instance, an Australian tells of his home-coming in these words: "I received a warm welcome from all except my own daughter, who turned me down absolutely. It took me six months to woo her, but now she owns me as her Daddy." Another, writing from Canada of the unforgettable drawing-room in London, and of the people he met there, speaks of "that ideal circle." They all speak of cherishing their memories, and describe how they tell their womanfolk of her unfailing goodness.

"Alone in London." To those who have met Mrs. Edwardes these words have no meaning. . . . We can never forget our reception; it was a continual home coming of a long-lost but most welcome son. London! —who can describe it?—and the country, with its abbeys, cathedrals, castles, country, and farmhouses, its grass and gardens. . . . Links have been forged that can never be broken.

One little matter in the hospitality of Mrs. Edwardes seems to me worthy of mention. At the outset, she who had originated this noble idea of personal hospitality to overseas officers decided to permit smoking in her drawing-room. This concession was an act of real sacrifice. Tobacco smoke affected her health. But somebody came to her and said: "You are wrong to allow smoking. It destroys the idea of a lady's drawing-room. It makes your hospitality that of a club or a hostel. The men prefer to feel that they are in an English home—in a lady's drawing-room." From that day smoking was restricted to a room on the ground floor, and those who mounted the stairs to the drawing-room did so for the pleasures of conversation. As Mrs. Edwardes knows a great number of people in society, and as everybody delights to do her honour, the soldiers of our Dominion met in that drawing-room some of the best representatives of English intellectual life, and many of the most charming women of the Old Guard in aristocracy.

Lady Harrowby observed the same rule about smoking in her house in Grosvenor Place. Soldiers from overseas found her to be one of the kindest and cheerfulest women in London, but a martinet in the matter of social manners. She does not smoke, and her drawing-room, filled with beautiful flowers and beautiful furniture, is not a smoking-room. She was delighted to crowd her room with soldiers, but for conversation, or music, or dancing. She showed them a room, with a balcony over the street, where smoking was allowed, and without an exception her guests gladly acquiesced in her rule.

The truth is that this little rule indicates very happily the idea which inspired all this boundless hospitality. It was the hospitality of the English home at its very best, and to this day, in the houses where the best traditions of English home life are observed, no one dreams of smoking in the drawing-room, and, moreover, the ladies themselves do not smoke. Let me confess that there have been times in my life when I have found this rule irksome; but let me also acknowledge with gratitude how keenly I have appreciated the sweet blessings of tobacco after the beneficent abstinence of several hours in a drawing-room.

Lady Harrowby is a philosopher in these matters. Her whole life has a thesis. She believes that every convention should be challenged for its *raison d'être*, but that, passing that challenge, each should be resolutely observed. This is to say, she regards the reasonable rules and regulations of society as beneficent; she holds that their observance is essential to the right-

ful tone of society and good for the discipline of individual character. She is firmly opposed to the anarchy of
licence; she is a stern unbending champion of restraint
and dignity.

Her spirit shows itself in her appearance; she is
tall and impressive, with something regal in her carriage,
her manner candid and frank, but not impulsive. All
her emotions are well under intellectual control. She
makes one feel how honest she is, how real, how straight,
how fearless, how willing to be kind and helpful; but
always, until intimacy is established, the dignity in her
presence seems to stand guard over the citadel of her
affections. It is only her closest friends who know how
loving Lady Harrowby can be.

The reader might suppose that a lady so formidable
and strict would perhaps rather frighten the overseas
Colonial soldier, freed from the awful inhumanity of the
trenches for a few days' leave in London—the London
so full of free and easy carnival for those with money in
their pockets. It shows, I think, how eminently the
heart of man is domestic, that a woman of Lady Harrowby's character should have made a profound impression
on her guests. They loved coming to her house. She
and her daughter (the two ladies are like sisters) became
in the eyes of thousands of Colonial soldiers ideal
representatives of English social life at its best—a
life of warmth, friendliness, and bright good cheer,
but a life of refinement, virtue, good manners, moral

sweetness, and great social dignity. I mean, these men from every quarter of the Empire, and drawn from almost every class of their various communities, found themselves not only perfectly at ease in Lady Harrowby's house, but perfectly happy in that atmosphere of sweetness and restraint, where an attitude of reverence towards women was as natural as irreverence in a night-club.

But of this let some of the letters speak:

We all look upon you as a personal friend.

I'd willingly go through the black nightmare of Ypres again for all the kindness I have received since I returned.

I am off to France this afternoon, and I really feel I have much more to fight for than ever before.

You open your houses to us and you ask us to your table. By doing so you lay us under a chivalrous obligation to rise to the best that we feel and know within ourselves, and so you bring out, perhaps without knowing it, the best that is in us.

Do not for one moment ever doubt the value morally and religiously of your work.

The thought one has about all this is how to make some return. Probably such a return can be best made in France!

When we get back to Australia, one of the memories of England that will be very dear to us, and which we will not want to forget, is the welcome that the homes of England have given to the Colonials.

Your reward is the knowledge that you have given so many of us "Home Life," kept us straight, and, above all, helped to keep the Empire together.

The other night our Colonel spoke about what the

7

British women had done and were doing. He called for three cheers for them, and I wish you could have heard it. It was some prolonged noise.

Finally, let this letter written by an Australian lady witness to the relief and gratitude which came to the mothers and wives of Dominion soldiers on hearing of their visits to Lady Harrowby and her friends.

What I want to assure you of is the deep gratitude we Australian women feel towards those women in England who are good to our boys. Not to be able to see them on furlough, to nurse them when ill, to comfort them when limbs and eyes were lost, to feel 12,000 miles of separation, is breaking our women. They just close their eyes and work. . . .

It is invaluable, your work. None of these men to whom you have been so kind will ever again feel anything but warm friendly gratitude to English people. . . . Deep in our hearts, I think, we all judge a nation by its home life.

In the case of Lady Harrowby's home life, its business activity must have impressed the Dominion soldier. Lady Frances Ryder, for example, was not only the principal driving force in her mother's work of organising hospitality, but she was also secretary to the A. D. M. S. of Australia in the matter of convalescent leave for officers of the A. I. F. and exercised the greatest personal care in finding suitable hostesses in all specially difficult cases. Her activity was the wonder of her friends and the admiration of the Dominion soldiers.

It is characteristic of Lady Harrowby that she makes light of her own share in this work. She ascribes all the glory to the hosts and hostesses who received Dominion officers into their country houses and entertained them for days and weeks. She says that she was merely the secretary of this tremendous work, too absorbed in organisation, too busy finding hostesses all over the country, to become in any real sense a friend of so many men. But there are some people who make a deep impression on our minds merely by the moral atmosphere which surround them, merely by the sense of goodness and sweetness which emanates from their presence; and Lady Harrowby, for all her strenuous work of organisation, being one of those well-poised spirits whom no crisis can overset, no emergency can fuss, had only to appear in her drawing-room, only to pass through an apartment filled with soldiers from France, only to smile upon her guests, to touch their lives with a grace which they welcomed. The letters of officers from all parts of the Empire speak again and again of this gratitude for her *personal* kindness, and one perceives all through these letters a feeling of pride and gladness that Lord and Lady Harrowby treated their writers as rational and moral beings, not as mere children to be amused, and deemed them worthy of a friendship which never descended to the easy levels below intellectual and spiritual refinement.

Mr. Charles Hill, a devoted and self-sacrificing

worker, who paid thousands of visits to hospitals, convalescent homes, and hostels, seeking for Dominion soldiers, and who came into contact with many of the ladies in Lady Harrowby's organisation, told me a story which illustrates the difficulties encountered by these ladies in entertaining their guests.

He said to me: "I was once visiting the Third London Hospital at Wandsworth, speaking of a visit that I was organising to Apsley House. A young officer said to me, 'I'd like to go there awfully, for my great-grandfather was an ensign at Waterloo!' Unfortunately, when the day came, he was too ill for the outing.

"I mentioned the matter to Lady Hilda Murray, who spends her whole day in doing kindnesses, and is never too busy to do an extra one—I don't know how she manages it. The idea of this descendant of a Waterloo ensign touched her. She told me later that she had arranged for him to visit Apsley House, and that Lady Eileen Orde would be there to show him over alone. I could not go on that day, for I was taking a party down to Penshurst, but I showed the boy where the house stood, told him how lucky he was, and explained that he had only to ring the bell of Apsley House to see all its contents, including the wonderful museum.

"On my return in the evening I encountered this young officer. I asked him how he had enjoyed his visit. He replied that he hadn't gone. He made a blushing excuse, something about not having noticed how time was going till the clock struck twelve. I asked him if he had telephoned to Lady Eileen. No. Had he telegraphed? No. Ought he to have done so? he asked. The truth is, the poor boy, dying to go, was too nervous to face a great house alone. Many of them, asked to a London house, got no further than the door. We had to take them and introduce them to their hostesses. Once the ice was broken, they were perfectly at their ease, and went again and again. But the shyness of these great strong lads was something to wonder at. A duchess seemed to them ever so much more alarming than a battery of German guns. Their modesty was really charming."

It was the naturalness, rather than the tact, of our best English ladies which won the confidence of these young giants. They did not want rackety women. They were not seeking the Bohemianism of the "smart set." They wanted home life at its zenith, home life as centuries of noble traditions have made it, and once past its imposing portals, once introduced into the natural sweetness of that interior, they were at their ease. None of them ever lost his reverence for our best women, but all were surprised to find how friendly and gracious a thing is human excellence.

Of one woman, Mrs. Graham Murray, who gave herself up to this work with an extreme of self-sacrifice, I should like to make a particular mention. Mrs. Graham Murray presided over the destinies of Peel House, which was used as a club for private soldiers from our Dominions. She lived there. It contained 600 beds. Occasionally it was a little noisy. She maintained an absolute hold, however, over the affections of her lodgers. She organised for these men visits to cathedrals under the care of architects, arranged river picnics for them, got them tickets for theatres, sent them sightseeing all over London. Worked to death, she would, nevertheless, go off at the call of the telephone to play the piano for officers from the Dominions who wanted to dance in one of the big London houses. Very often, in the small hours of the morning, she would find no taxicab to take her back to Peel House, and would have to drag herself there all the way on foot.

Once, tired out and fit for nothing, she saw an intoxicated Colonial soldier in Regent Street, arguing with a policeman, and in peril of the sharks of the street. She went to him, got him away, and persuaded him to let her lead him to Peel House. At the end of the dreary walk the maudlin soldier thanked her for seeing him home, and offered her sixpence. The scandalised doorkeeper intervened. "Do you know who that lady is?" "No." "It's the Honourable Mrs. Graham Murray!" The soldier plunged his hand into his pocket. "Well, give her a pound!" he said, and dragged out a grubby note.

Mrs. Graham Murray worked like a slave for this country's good name during the War, and her quite splendid and continuous service made less noise in the world than one of the charity bazaars at Albert Hall, where Fashion played at being unselfish.

If I had the space, I should like to write about the work for Overseas War Guests, notably the club at Norfolk House, most generously given by the Duchess of Norfolk, for ladies from our Dominions. This club numbered 3,300 guests; there was no subscription, concerts and lectures were given free, meals were served at cost price. The members, gathered from every part of the Empire, greatly valued the historic character of their splendid premises, and invited their men-folk to various entertainments in those beautiful rooms. But this work, linked up with hospitality to Dominion officers, and homes for women workers from the Dominions, deserves a volume to itself. It was one of the really great works done for the Empire—great because it had the touch of domesticity; it brought the women of the Empire together as nothing else could have done.

Among other women of my acquaintance who did not play at war work, but who threw themselves into this work with a sincere devotion and who are still doing work of national importance, are Miss Meriel Talbot, Mrs. Alfred Lyttelton, and Lady Sybil Grey, figures almost unknown in plutocratic circles, but English-women of the first class, all of them with an intimate knowledge of the British Empire.

It is instructive to observe that the spirit of war

work still continues to animate the activities of good women. Lady Hilda Murray, one of the most charming people in London, is as energetic as ever in her work of imperial consolidation; and Lady Frances Ryder has an organisation for showing personal hospitality, both in London and the country, to the great number of Dominion students now in England. Lady Limerick has set up an Ex-Service Men's Club in Dartford, in Kent, which might well serve as a model to every city and town throughout the country.

Lady Limerick's wonderful work during the War deserves something more than a passing reference. She is one of those impulsive and emotional women, who at first slightly disturb the habitual placidity of the Anglo-Saxon, but after a little while her absolute self-abnegation, her utter devotion to other people, and her tumultuous enthusiasm for all that is kindly and warm and generous, rather sweeps one away, and makes one wonder whether our political problems would not surrender to solution more quickly and easily if we approached them in this liberal spirit of loving-kindness. Perhaps we are too cold, too formal, too afraid of trusting our intellects, of which we are not very sure, in a strong tide of genuine emotion.

At the outset of War, Lady Limerick had a personal encounter with a soldier at Victoria Station which led her to think of giving all her time to these men. Miss Hildyard, soon after this event, began a work of hospitality at this station; before Lady Limerick could take any part in it, Mrs. Matthews had set a great machinery in motion which never ceased to run till the end of the War. Accordingly, Lady Limerick went off to London Bridge with her friend Mrs. Butler, and in this windiest of London stations, with its high levels and low levels, its endless stairs and its winding passages, set up a free buffet for soldiers, which became one of the friendliest things on the home front. At the end of the War she had ministered to seven and a half million soldiers.

This gigantic undertaking, so easily forgotten, so difficult to maintain, was carried on from beginning to end with only one paid worker, a charwoman. Among those who gave their services, and worked like galley slaves by day and by night, one relief missing luncheon, the other dinner, were many of the first women in the land. I can find room to name only a few of these devoted ladies, who were on their feet for long hours, and who had no fire to warm them in winter, and whose snatched meals consisted chiefly of tea and sandwiches. Lady Limerick would place first on her list Queen Alexandra, because the occasional presence of this gracious lady not only put heart into her staff, but gave such extraordinary pleasure to the soldiers coming and going from the front. Their cheers for Queen Alexandra, she tells me, ring in her ears to this day.

Among the other ladies, some of whom never missed a

single day all those years, were Lady Evelyn Farquhar (who greatly distinguished herself during a bad air raid), Miss Sonia Keppel (a most devoted worker), Lady Betty Butler, Lady Hugh Grosvenor, Lady Lister-Kaye, Lady Poultney, Lady Rossmore, Lady Evelyn Ward, Lady Milbanke, Lady Bingham, the Hon. Mrs. John Ward, and many other ladies too numerous to mention. Their great work never failed. The free buffet at London Bridge became a real memory in the life of seven and a half million soldiers; the spirit of it was so warm and so friendly.

Lady Limerick once had a slight altercation with a staff colonel, who seemed to resent her motherly manner with soldiers, not knowing who she was or anything of her work. "Ah!" she cried, with mock derision, "you're too English to feel like a human being." "I'm from Tipperary," said the colonel. "Are you, though?" "I am." "Well, then, 'tis a long time since you were there." At the end of all her disputes she has the habit of saying, "Me name's Limerick, and I'm from Ireland, though you mightn't think it from me accent." A great-hearted, motherly woman, on whom sorrow has rained the most terrible sufferings, but whose spirit is unbowed, and whose heart is full of the music of humanity.

I will conclude this chapter with a reference to work of quite a different kind, a branch of which was carried on during the War by Mrs. John Thynne, and is still being carried on—the work of rescuing fallen women. I remember going to Mrs. Thynne's house during the War, and meeting there her friend, Princess Christian, and several other people gathered together to discuss this most difficult question. Not all the terrible distractions of the struggle in France could deflect Mrs. Thynne from this narrow path of duty which she has faithfully and most courageously followed for fifty years. The War rendered her work more difficult, more heart-breaking, but Mrs. Thynne and her friends were determined to meet the increased difficulties by extra efforts and extra courage.

It is interesting to know that Mrs. Thynne was drawn into this work as a young bride in 1873 by Lady Augusta Stanley, of whom Mr. Birrell gives us a momentary glance in his charming monograph on Frederick Locker-Lampson. Lady Augusta was characteristically English in the central seriousness of character from which radiated all her social brightness. The argument she used to the beautiful Mrs. Thynne was a simple one; it is the duty of happy married women to help girls who are forlorn and friendless—happiness is a responsibility. In this way it came about that one of the sweetest young brides in London was to be seen in the seventies moving through the shadows of London midnight streets, speaking to fallen women, and taking those who would come with her to houses of rescue. And from that day to this, with scores of women definitely saved from destruction by her efforts, Mrs. Thynne has never abandoned her labour of love.

The Gladstones had long been at this work; perhaps it was through them that Lady Edward Cavendish and Lady Sarah Spencer, unknown to their parents, would go to their rooms in the midst of a great reception at Devonshire House, or after a dinner-party, and change their fine frocks for dark garments, and then steal out into the streets to attempt the rescue of fallen women. Mrs. Thynne knows this to be true, and a great friend of mine who scouted it at first has since confirmed it. Mrs. Thynne tells me that many great ladies gave themselves to this bitter work, but in most cases did it in secret.

She tells me of the help she herself received from Adeline, Duchess of Bedford, who visited prisons, and sought by preventive work of many kinds to stem the tide of harlotry. I knew the duchess, and know how good she was, and I am quite certain she laboured heart and soul in this direction; but, unhappily she lacked the beautiful naturalness of her sister, Lady Henry Somerset, and had none of that gentle sweetness which makes Mrs. Thynne irresistible. Her influence in society would have been far greater if she had possessed something of the richness of Lady Limerick's emotionalism. She was a good woman, but her nature, not her heart, was cold. She could never give herself;

her life, yes, but not herself. Perhaps it was an inner timidity that held her captive.

Among the other people whose preventive work during the War saved thousands of young girls from ruin, Mrs. Thynne mentions the Dowager Lady Hillingdon, Francis Lady de l'Isle and Dudley, Lady St. Cyres, and the Duchess of Atholl, all of whom saw to it that no red tape encumbered their ministrations. To these ladies, of whose activities the public knows nothing, we owe it that many thousands of girl war-workers were brought into close personal contact with influences of a pure and refining nature. No statistics of such work can tell its story. The nation may be certain, however, that because of these good women, purity held its own at a time when no immodesty seemed greatly to matter.

How little we know of the goodness in the world! The other day, lunching at St. James's Palace, I met an elderly gentleman whom I had often seen before, but to whom I had never been introduced. I knew him as one who goes about a good deal, and is warmly liked by his Eton contemporaries, in whose houses he is a constant guest. This elderly gentleman, may I be allowed to say, is remarkable for no gifts; he is not a brilliant conversationalist, has no store of anecdotes and quotations at his command, is not in any sense of the word a "performer." He is remarkable only for a singular benignity of manner and a charming kindliness of expression.

A friend of mine to whom I happened to mention this

encounter asked me if I knew about Mr.—'s life, and then told me the following story:

"He lives alone in a little street which has many shabby corners, looked after by an old butler and an old cook, who have been with him for forty years. He used to give the most charming little dinners, but taxation and the high price of things have put an end to this hospitality. But the War did not put an end to his other kindnesses. He has a district in Whitechapel which he visits regularly, calling on old people in their little houses, just as he calls on ladies in this part of the town. He does not preach, distribute tracts, or argue as a political propagandist; he is a social visitor to these old bodies, calling to inquire after their health and patiently listening to their gossip. Once every week he takes a blind man for a walk. There is a hospital in London to which he goes to talk to the patients who have no visitors. He has been a constant friend to St. Dunstan's. Very few people in London know anything about this part of his life. They simply regard him as a charming old bachelor, who has looked on at the pageant of social life from a snug corner. But he is really one of the kindest and most unselfish of men—a lovable man, full of gentleness and sympathy."

What a portrait of an English gentleman!

As I think of all the good work done during and since the War—think of Sir Arthur Pearson's work for blind soldiers and blind children—I feel that this chapter will never come to an end. Yet I must turn to my main subject, which is constructive criticism, though I have mentioned but a tithe of all that devoted service.

In concluding this chapter, however, I would like to pay tribute to the zeal and self-sacrificing labours of those ladies who never wearied in bringing consolation and assistance to the widows of fallen officers, young women often left suddenly without a friend in the world, or a shilling in their purses. Among these ministering women were Lady Lansdowne, Lady Hope (daughter of the beautiful and witty Lady Constance Leslie) and Mrs. Brinton, better known as Mrs. William James. Mrs. Brinton truly worked like a Trojan, and I know how often she went long journeys at great trouble and expense to comfort some poor young mother left suddenly destitute. But she likes to hide her personal work, and to ascribe the increasing success of the Officers' Families Association to the businesslike chairmanship of Princess Christian, and to the devotion of ladies like Mrs. Austen Chamberlain who serve on the committee. Homes are provided for these widows and their babies at a merely nominal rent, and the Association does all that is possible in the matter of educating the children. Perhaps something of the tragedy of this work may be realised when it is known that many widows of young officers found themselves without a penny to buy mourning, their pay stopped, their pensions not granted. This great work, carried on throughout the War, is still being carried on with devotion and personal sacrifice.

But now I really must turn this page—so delightful to write, but so inadequate to the labours it attempts to describe if only in the finest of thin outlines. The reader in foreign countries, particularly, I hope, in the United States, will agree with me, however, in spite of this sketchiness, that there is a side to English society which is neither base nor contemptible.

In my conclusion to this book I am going to argue that goodness is not enough, and to suggest that the Aristotelian idea of a Higher Excellence than morality is essential to the development of a true and powerful aristocracy. But for the present I seek only to undo, as far as it is possible so late in the day, some of the ill consequences of books like Mrs. Asquith's and Colonel Repington's, not pretending for a moment that English aristocracy meets the full needs of the time, but contending that it is not wholly false to its traditions and not wholly unmindful of its duties.

MRS. GLADSTONE AT HAWARDEN

1893

From a portrait by J. McLure Hamilton

CHAPTER VIII

MANNERS

Consider these people, then, their way of life, their habits, their manners, the very tones of their voices; look at them attentively; observe the literature they read, the things which give them pleasure, the words which come forth out of their mouths, the thoughts which make the furniture of their minds; would any amount of wealth be worth having with the condition that one was to become just like these people by having it?—MATTHEW ARNOLD.

LET us now return to our study of Fashion, seeking to discover in what respects it fails the English people, and does harm to the orderly evolution of English civilisation.

Lady Frances Balfour declared of Mrs. Asquith's book that "licence in manners must not be confused with a licence in morals"; and I suppose the vast majority of people will agree with her in thus separating morals from manners, and thus degrading manners below the level of morals.

Nevertheless, this condition of mind is fatal to human progress.

To suggest that morals are more important than

manners is equivalent to asserting that the Greek alphabet is more important than the Dialogues of Plato. Morals are the study of the kindergarten. They proceed out of lessons on the use of tooth-brush and flannel. When we teach men not to steal, and not to murder, we are instructing them only in the elements of conduct. The Sermon on the Mount was not a plagiarism of Sinai nor a paraphrase of the Tables of Stone; it was in an altogether different region—it was a discourse on manners.

It is when we have left the kindergarten of the moral life, and have entered the university of the spiritual life, that we proceed from the Ten Commandments to gentleness, mercy, humility, sweetness, self-abnegation, love; and not until we have graduated in manners may we call ourselves without absurdity citizens of civilisation.

Many people have been shocked by Nietzsche's statement that if the kingdom of righteousness and peace was established on earth, it would mean "a kingdom of the profoundest mediocrity and Chinaism." But a greater than Nietzsche said the same thing. The righteousness of the Pharisee was condemned by Jesus, perfect as that righteousness was, because it could lead only to stagnation—that is to say, to mediocrity and Chinaism.

To announce "Here is the law, and obedience to the law satisfies the universe," is to close the one door on

earth which life has been able to keep open for the
eternal struggle after infinite improvement.   It is necessary, if that one door on earth is to be kept open, to say,
"Be ye perfect, even as your Father in heaven is perfect."   Man can no more stop at morality than the
elephant can go forward to mathematics or music.
It is essential to the whole scheme of things that man
should have an open road for his progress.   When he
has learned not to rob his neighbour, and not to kill
those who possess things which he covets, he has
passed from the savage, but has by no means reached
manhood.   The police-court is not a rehearsal of the
Judgment Day, nor is the gate of heaven guarded by
an official from Scotland Yard.

> All indistinctly apprehend a bliss
> On which the soul may rest; the hearts of all
> Yearn after it, and to that wished bourne
> All therefore strive.

Because of the grave importance of this matter,
I hope I may be forgiven if I express the hope that
the Prince of Wales, who can do so much for the nation
if he will take the next step on the road to spiritual
development, will not mistake popularity for influence.
It is of high importance to the Empire that his staff
should consist of men whose intelligence is equal to
their social position.   To be charming is a great power,
and a tremendous responsibility.   With his nature,

which is so attractive, the Prince may do a great deal to save society from a grave disaster. He will best serve the nation in this way if he makes friends only among the best men and women of the day, its scholars and its workers, those people whose lives are devoted to the highest interests of the human race, and whose culture entitles them to be the leaders of English civilisation. It is possible, perhaps, for a Prince of Wales to be too familiar a figure, too often the centre of a vast crowd; certainly it is of high importance that he should have the most ample leisure for conversation with the first minds of the world. From him, more than from anybody of our time, is the next generation likely to draw its idea of manners.

The idea that manners are merely the accomplishment of a class, or an indication of one's place in the social hierarchy, or something that has to do with etiquette and ceremonial—this perversion of truth has not, perhaps, as numerous a constituency as its fellow falsehood, that money is a key to happiness. But that a woman so good and so clever as Lady Frances Balfour should say a word tending to propagate this destructive falsehood reveals to all who care for England, and who believe that the tone of English life is infinitely more important than parliamentary enactments, in how perilous a position we have come to stand.

We are talking nonsense on the edge of an abyss.

If you would see the truth of this matter, study the Founder of Christianity, whose manners permeated if they did not create English character.

Morals, with Christ, had to do with man as he was; Manners with what He was becoming. His blessing was on the springs of behaviour—on meekness and gentleness, on humility and lowliness, on hunger and thirst after perfection, on mercy, purity of heart, and long suffering.

When He stooped and wrote in the dust, He was overcome, not by the sin of the captured woman, but by the morality of her accusers, a morality so earnest and triumphant that it took no count of the sinner's feelings, was unconscious even of wounding her sense of delicacy.

His manner to those who were guilty of a licence in morals was invariably gentle and tender; on the other hand, the mere sight of a Pharisee moved Him to an indignation which sometimes disturbed the central serenity of His nature.

His teaching took the Ten Commandments for granted. His text began with manners and proceeded to perfection.

St. Paul summed up this teaching in a hymn of such exquisite beauty that no words of Shakespeare so haunt the human mind: "Though I speak with the tongues of men and of angels, and have not charity, I am become as sounding brass, or a tinkling cymbal."

What has the universe got to do with sounding brass and a tinkling cymbal? He might perform every requirement of the law, even to the extreme of giving all his goods to the poor and his body to be burned, and yet be worth nothing.

If ever any instruction was plain and simple, it is this instruction of Christ that spiritual evolution, spiritual growth, turns on an attitude, a behaviour, a manner, a way of handling life, of regarding the universe.

This was His revelation. Morality can destroy a soul quite as easily as immorality. Indeed, the destruction of morality is greater, for it hardens the heart; that is to say, hardens the point of contact with God. But with love in the heart, the soul even of a great sinner is not lost to the purposes of creation. It is certain that the angels would prefer to see the earth inhabited by a single human being after the pattern of David or Augustine than crowded in every continent with Pharisees.

Mrs. Asquith drew up a summary of her history and her aspirations. The last of those aspirations was for "a crowded memorial service." Will Lady Frances Balfour defend the vulgarity of soul which inspired that aspiration? Is there not in this passion for a last crowd, as it were a last audience, something that shocks us in the depths of our nature more than the sins of the weak and the uneducated?

Much is to be learned from that flippancy. Does

it not witness to an immense desolation of the woman's heart? She does not dare to be alone with herself even in the grave. She would have the fashionable world, and the photographers of the illustrated papers, as near her coffin as burial will permit. As the tree falls, so would it lie. As she has sown, so would she reap. What vulgarity!

I think the decline in manners is to be atrributed to a single cause—the loss in man of a sense of dignity. He has dislocated his spirit. It is no longer articulated with the universe. He thinks of himself as an animal, and of the earth as something unrelated to the rest of creation. Myopia has seen infinity and formulated a thesis of existence. We are outside the invisible; we have no connection with eternity; our terrestrial past is minus a meaning; the future of humanity is without a goal.

There was once on this earth a period known as the Drift Age. At the present moment we are witnessing a Drift Age in morals. Why should man be particular about learning his alphabet if the end is only to spell with those difficult letters the word Nothing?

Many people have a fear of Bolshevism. A more likely danger to overtake the human race is destruction by Pessimism. Moral languor means something more than a reversion to animalism; it means a descent into devilry.

In the sphere of manners I am convinced that the

example of Fashion makes powerfully for this danger of Pessimism.

Look at Fashion as it exhibits itself to mankind after a calamity unparalleled in history, and ask if its example in manners lends any encouragement to the passion of the man of science for knowledge, to the desire of the world for peace, to the belief of the spiritual that life is an everlasting evolution of beauty, power, and knowledge?

What end does Fashion offer to mankind for their labours? Its voice is lifted up to say, "Work hard if you would have a good time," and its good time is a condition of luxury. At the door of Fashion the sentinel does not challenge those who approach with the cry, "Who goes there?" but "How much do you bring?" So long as a man has made money, no matter in what way, and no matter how dull or how stupid or how flagrantly vulgar he may be, Fashion will open its door to him, and he is admitted to the Olympus of our national life. There are men on that Olympus at the present moment, boasting of their aristocratic friends, whose minds are as truly ignorant of culture as the mind of a Patagonian or an Esquimaux.

In *The Young Visiters*, at which the world has laughed with a rare delight, but which contains matter that might almost be said to be written for our learning, there is a conversation between Mr. Salteena and the Earl of Clincham in the Compartments of the Crystal

Palace which I think is perfectly characteristic of modern society.

Mr. Salteena desires to enter fashionable circles and presents himself before Lord Clincham, who inquires his name.   We read:

> Mr. Salteena seated himself gingerly on the edge of a crested chair.   To tell you the truth my Lord I am not anyone of import and I am not a gentleman as they say, he ended getting very red and hot.
> Have some whiskey said lord Clincham and he poured the liquid into a glass at his elbow.   Mr. Salteena lapped it up thankfully.
> . . . The Earl gave a slight cough and gazed at Mr. Salteena thourghtfully.
> Have you much money he asked and are you prepared to spend a good deal.
> Oh yes quite gasped Mr. Salteena.

We smile; but the pantomime is true to life.   Is there a living soul who doubts for a moment that aristocracy has sold the pass to Dives?   Is there, on the visible summit of our national life, we may fairly ask, even one true lineal descendant of that aristocracy in the sixteenth century which led the Renaissance?   We cannot pretend that we have a working aristocracy—an aristocracy, I mean, whose example penetrates and interpenetrates the social organism.   It would be foolish to make that pretence.   We possess in place of an aristocracy of culture a powerful and cynical plutocracy which is as wholly given to the worship of Mam-

mon as any nation of heathen times. It is this plutocracy which influences the whole social organism. At
the head of the nation are the Mammonites. Fashion
may amuse itself with the mime and the artist, but
its only heirs are the sons of Dives. No one, indeed,
can live in that world who is not rich. He may be
utterly ignorant, without grace, without value of any
kind for the higher life of humanity; but so long as he is
not poor, he marches at the head of the English nation.

This condition of modern society has a twofold effect
on the nation. On the great bulk of the English people
it has a vulgarising effect—it makes them think highly
of money and scornfully of culture, it makes them hot
for self-indulgence and cold towards self-development,
it makes them eager for parade, display, ostentation;
they have no inward life, they are "nowhere greater
strangers than at home," their eyes are in the ends of
the earth.

The other effect is on the wage-earner, whose rise
in wages is at almost every point defeated by the cost
of living; on him the display of the ostentatious rich has
an exasperating effect. At first he strives, like so many
of those above him, to imitate Fashion, but fails, becomes reckless, and takes to preaching a gospel of plun-
der and destruction.

Now, obviously, the one valid justification for an
aristocracy is that it should lead the nation in the right
way. It is of value to a state only when it uses its enor-

mous advantages to discourage what is vain or unprofit-
able in the social life of the nation, and to encourage
all that makes for lasting joy and the deepest satisfaction
of the human spirit.

Above everything else, it is the duty of an upper
class to set the highest example in manners. We
should be able to take the morals of an aristocracy
for granted. What we chiefly require of it is leadership
in manners—that is to say, in an attitude towards the
universe, a handling of life. If it teaches us that luxury
and ostentation are the chief goods of life, and that
the wise man is he who possesses himself of the means
for purchasing those goods, then clearly the Bolshevist
has as great encouragement for his thesis as the sweater
of labour, the swindler, the card-sharper, and the
burglar have for their methods. The whole struggle of
the nation must inevitably be towards the trough.

Fashion is so placed that it must set either a good
or a bad example to the nation. It cannot move without affecting the whole structure of society. Humanity looks up to Fashion, and is either deceived by it or
disgusted. Therefore, as I would persuade the central
classes of the nation to see, it is a matter vital to the
well-being of the community that Fashion should set
examples which strengthen the nation and inspire it to
noble living.

I would lay emphasis on the disastrous consequences
of ostentation. I believe that nothing makes the work

of the revolutionist easier than the ostentatious luxury of the rich. Its social consequence is bad enough, for it is vulgarising the middle classes in battalions; but its political consequence may well be worse than anything we have yet known in our history. Ostentation of the kind which is now rampant in the public circles of Fashion maddens the atheistical brain of the man who has, with a talent for declamation, a struggle to exist.

If there is one great and controlling principle in the behaviour of the average good Englishman it is the principle of reserve.

This virtue is not always the higher virtue of modesty, but it makes for that virtue. The characteristic Englishman does not advertise either his position or his possessions. He calls it very bad manners to dress loudly, to talk at the top of the voice, to make a display of jewellery, to conduct a household ostentatiously, to be pushful, noisy, extravagant, showy, and brazen; these things he regards as "bad form." They have no temptations for him. They are distasteful.

But among the rich on the summit of our national life this principle of behaviour, which I reckon to be the historic centre of English character, has no existence.

These vulgar people have used money to advertise their wares, and now would use the money made by that advertisement to advertise themselves. The shop window is transferred from commercial to social life. Reserve in business would be ruin; reserve in social life would be suicide. As they attracted the public to buy their goods, so they would attract aristocracy to a knowledge of their arrival in Vanity Fair. They advertise their existence by hanging their women with jewels, by building palatial houses, and by giving entertainments which in every detail flash wealth in the eyes of their parasitic guests.

"Me's here!" is the announcement of Midas, striding into the Olympus of English life, and Fashion hurries forward to offer a "crested chair."

Ostentation, this disease which threatens our destruction, is not a crime which brings the policeman after those who spread its contagion; it is not nearly so great a thing in the eyes of the moralist as the liquor question or the question of harlotry; it is in truth a breach of manners, a mere vanity against which the Almighty set no canon in the thunders of Sinai, a thing to be expected, a matter for the gentle ridicule of *Punch*, an affair beneath the notice of Parliament and Church.

Nevertheless it is a bad example—an example not of low morals, but of bad manners, and an example which many will follow who would resist an example in bad morals; so it comes about that we are moving in mass on a road so wholly opposite to the road marked out for our advance that we cannot hope, if we persist in following it, to escape the wilderness.

It is curious how the true nature of fine manners can escape the attention of even very intelligent people.

I find this passage concerning the eighties in that very interesting and ably-written book *The Reminiscences of Lady Randolph Churchill:*

> Etiquette and the amenities of social life were thought much more of then than now.   The writing of ceremonious notes, the leaving of cards, not to speak of *visites de digestion,* which even young men were supposed to pay, took up most afternoons.   There was little or none of that extraordinary restlessness and craving for something new which is a feature of to-day, necessarily causing manners to deteriorate, and certainly curtailing the amenities of social life on which past generations set such store.   A nod replaces the ceremonious bow, a familiar handshake the elaborate curtsey.   The carefully worded, beautifully written invitation of thirty years ago is dropped in favour of a garbled telephone message such as "Will Mrs. S. dine with Lady T., and bring a man; and if she can't find one she mustn't come, as it would make them thirteen"; or a message to a club: "Will Mr. G. dine with Lady T. to-night?   If so, will he look in the card-room and see if any of her lot are there, and suggest somebody."   Life, however, seemed to be as full then as it is now, although people did not try to press into one day the duties and pleasures of a week, finishing none and enjoying none.   The motor and the telephone were unknown, and the receipt of the shilling telegram was still unusual enough to cause feelings of apprehension.   There was none of that easy tolerance and familiarity which is undoubtedly fostered by the daily, not to say hourly, touch and communication of modern society.

The idea in the writer's mind seems to be that manners are merely a sort of social polish, a grace of the body as it were, like a distinguished diction or a pleasantness in conversation.   But manners, rightly regarded, are the *style of the soul*, and they can never be genuine, never be anything more than veneer or polish, unless they proceed as naturally as the exhalation of a rose from the inmost beauty of the spirit, that is to say, from humility, tenderness, loving-kindness, and desire of excellence.

The reader of *The Mirrors of Downing Street* may remember that I ventured to criticise Mr. Arthur Balfour, passing behind the shield of his engaging and attractive manners to the central egoism of his character.   I was vehemently attacked for this criticism, one of my critics citing as a witness against me Mr. E. T. Raymond, who had just then published a biography of Mr. Balfour.

Apparently the only criticism to be gathered from that volume, in the opinion of this vehement gentleman, is that "Mr. Balfour fails in energy."   As for meanness, "there is not a trace of meanness in Mr. Balfour's nature, though there may be a touch of callousness."

It is difficult to believe that this declaration was delivered after reading a book which contains the story of Mr. Balfour's dealings with Mr. Ritchie, Lord George Hamilton, and Lord Balfour of Burleigh—that episode in which, to get rid of those chafing Free Traders, he hid from the knowledge of every member of his Cabinet, with the solitary exception of the honest and bewildered Duke of Devonshire, whom he desired to keep, the all-important fact that he had Mr. Joseph Chamberlain's resignation in his pocket.

In *The Mirrors of Downing Street* I did not go so far as to tell this story in full; I merely suggested it; but here it is, in the volume which my critic uses to vindicate Mr. Balfour's character, told as stolidly as any policeman could tell in the witness-box the story of a three-card trick.

What else does Mr. Raymond say of Mr. Balfour? He tells us that this patriotic statesman, this disinterested great gentleman, who is so indifferent to place and power, "could ill endure the comradeship of equals," and that in forming a Cabinet, a *Cabinet to be charged with the destinies of the British Empire*, he "took care, with regard to his own appointments, not to encourage men who could by any possibility threaten his position."

He was compared, about the time of Mr. Churchill's secession, to a beech-tree: very beautiful, but nothing could grow under its shade.

Mr. Raymond proceeds:

As the older politicians, the Goschens and Hicks-Beaches, dropped out, he filled their places with those who, through character, mind, or circumstance, were likely to develop no inconvenient individuality. Whether it was his brother, or his kinsman, or his friend whom he elevated, the understanding was the same; they were to be less Ministers of the Crown than retainers of Mr. Balfour.

Here is another paragraph:

> Not for the first time or the last in his life he overdid
> things through simple ignorance of the sensitiveness of
> the populace where it suspects any breach of the English
> tradition of fair play.

And this:

> Mr. Balfour could trust nobody; it is only fair to add
> that very few trusted him.

What, then, is the value of Mr. Balfour's manners?

As for Mr. Raymond, I take the liberty of saying
he would have arrived at a truer measure of his hero had
his knees not crooked quite so obviously in approaching
this "exquisite Aramis of politics." He has written
an indictment, but with a trembling hand. At the end,
rather horrified by what he has done, he throws up his
trembling hands with the exclamation, "What a strange
and elusive personality!" This is not judgment, it is
surrender.

To the true historian no personality is elusive.
He measures all by the same standard, looking at them,
not to see what interesting things he can say about these
candidates for Olympus, but only to take their true and
absolute measure. He asks of each one of them: "Was
this man truthful? Was he earnest? Was he unselfish?" And then he looks at the man's work, and
asks "Did it enrich the poor, comfort the sorrowful,
strengthen the weak, inspire the strong? Did it bring

9

glory to his nation, and peace to mankind?   What did
it accomplish for the higher life of the human race?''

Measure Mr. Balfour by the same standards with
which history has measured Abraham Lincoln, Mazzini,
and Gladstone, and where is his place among the
immortals?

The more we consider his charm, his powers, and his
advantages the greater must be our condemnation.
For every man's achievement should be judged by two
things—his gifts and his opportunities.

One of the traits in Mr. Balfour's character to which
I drew attention in *The Mirrors of Downing Street* was
his indifference to his servants.   Mr. Raymond makes
a very interesting reply to this criticism:

> Not knowing how he treats his servants, I have not
> accused him of treating them badly.
> I take it there are only two ways of getting accurate
> knowledge of such a point.   One must have been a
> servant of Mr. Balfour, or one must have been on con-
> fidential terms with a servant of Mr. Balfour.   Never
> having worn the Whittingeham livery, never having had
> a friend who has worn that livery, his personality in this
> regard has certainly eluded me.   But I am not in the least
> ashamed of omitting from an appraisement of Mr. Balfour
> the point of view of the servants' hall.

It will be observed that Mr. Raymond expresses in
this passage a contempt for servants.   That is important.   I pass over his obviously vain suggestion that a
man can tell how his friends and acquaintances treat

their servants only by becoming one of those servants
himself. I pass over this in order to lay particular
stress on the very repellent attitude to domestic
servants which Mr. Raymond strikes in this passage,
evidently in the belief that he is thoroughly in the
fashion, as indeed he is, but without realising that it is a
thoroughly bad new fashion. [1]

For myself, I gratefully acknowledge, I spent the
most Arcadian part of my boyhood in the company
of grooms and gamekeepers, that I loved an old country
nurse far more than my grandmothers and aunts, that
I paid innumerable visits to the kitchen, every feature
of which still lives affectionately in my mind, in order to
get sweet things from a most delightful old cook, and
also to see a quite elderly laundry woman perform
the astounding trick of jumping from the seat of a chair
over its back. Nor did my parents ever forbid my
brothers and me from accepting invitations to tea in
her cottage, most kindly offered to us by the coachman's
wife. In fact, looking back on those early years, I
seem to remember, much more clearly than the people
of my own class, the characters and personalities of
my father's servants and the villagers who surrounded
us, particularly the poachers, in whose cottages we were

[1] Mr. Wilfred Blunt records a conversation with Mr. Hyndman on
the subject of Winston Churchill. "They tell me," said Mr. Hyndman, "he is rude and brutal with servants." Mr. Blunt assured him
that this was not so, "and he was glad to hear it." Both these men are
gentlemen (*My Diaries*, Part II., p.306.).

always made extremely welcome, no matter what was the state of our boots.

This may seem shocking, or even unbelievable, to Mr. Raymond. But I would assure him few things were more charmingly characteristic of the old-fashioned English home than the affectionate relations which existed between the family and its faithful servants. The beautiful old Duchess of Abercorn, for example, was known to go rat-hunting with a stable boy even when she was ninety years of age, and there was not a servant in her house with whose family affairs she was not perfectly and even affectionately acquainted. Lord Lansdowne, as Governor-General of Canada, had one of his footmen as a curler in the Rideau Hall team. Mr. G. W. E. Russell had no truer friends than his butler and his cook, Mr. and Mrs. George Payne, to whom he bequeathed almost everything he possessed. One of the Wyndham boys is described by Mr. Blunt on a visit to Clouds in the following manner: "He is very good-looking, and spends most of his time with the servants in the pantry and the housekeeper's room, where he talks nonsense to the maids, and helps the footmen to clean the knives." And of the other children at Clouds we read: "They spent the day making a grand picnic with the servants and governesses." Mr. Samuel Butler lavished his affections on no one so completely as his servant Alfred, whose place in history is more secure than Mr. Raymond's. Perhaps Mr. Raymond, who is a journalist, will be more astonished by the following incident. I remember speaking to Lord Northcliffe on one occasion of a very intelligent footman who acted as my valet at Sutton Place. Lord Northcliffe, who is entirely free from all snobbishness, replied with enthusiasm: "I'm so glad you've talked to him. He's a very clever young fellow. I'm helping him in his education. I rather think he will do something in the world."

This matter of the treatment of servants is worthy of mention, because one of the worst characteristics of modern manners is a spirit of selfishness, conceit, and snobbishness which more and more tends to separate the various classes of the community. It is a spirit which entirely destroys the idea of the human family. *We are ceasing to think of others.*

Lord Frederic Hamilton has noticed this change in *The Days Before Yesterday:*[1]

Neither my father nor my mother ever dined out on Sunday, nor did they invite people to dinner on that day, for they wished to give those in their employment a day of rest. All quite hopelessly Victorian! for, after all, why should people ever think of anybody but themselves?

Present-day hostesses tell me that all young men, and most girls, are kind enough to flick cigarette ash all over their drawing-rooms, and considerately throw lighted cigarette-ends on the fine old Persian carpets, and burn holes in pieces of valuable old French furniture. Of

[1] *The Days Before Yesterday*, by Lord Frederic Hamilton.

course it would be too much trouble to fetch an ash-tray, or to rise to throw lighted cigarette-ends into the grate. The young generation have never been brought up to take trouble, nor to consider other people.

There you have the root cause of all bad manners, whatever form they take—*selfishness*.   And selfishness, what is it, if we examine it with attention, but a deep and most disfiguring *spiritual* defect?

As soon as we realise this truth, we perceive at once that manners—the word Hobbes employed for morals —are something much more important to the social and political life of a great nation than the physical graces offered to mankind at the hands of a professor in deport-ment.   They are the style of a nation—the mark it is making on the civilised progress of mankind.

But instead of a beautiful and noble life, a life leading upward from one spiritual desire to another, upward and onward to Dante's indistinctly apprehended bliss on which the soul may rest, instead of this we have at present the life of the jazz, the life of the Victory Dance.   Mr. Noyes has described this new form of the social rout, this new spirit of the national life, in memor-able verses, of which I am permitted by his publishers, Messrs. Cassell, to print one:

> The cymbals crash,
>   And the dancers walk,
> With long silk stockings
>   And arms of chalk,

Butterfly skirts,
And white breasts bare,
And shadows of dead men
Watching 'em there.

Sir Ian Hamilton, heartbroken by the Peace of
Versailles, has published in the John Keats Memorial
Volume an even more scornful indictment.   He speaks
of the angel who led our boyhood to the sacrifice of their
lives, an angel of spiritual exaltation, and then of
Versailles, where "the diplomats danced with their
typists." His soul rebels against this anti-climax.
The banners of self-sacrifice have been dragged through
the dirt.   The names of the valiant dead are writ in
water.

"Who has quenched that new star of Bethlehem
which still throughout the War went before the fighters
giving them some respite from their pain?   Why is it
that peace has suddenly made the vaulted heavens
as black as the socket from which some fiend has torn
the eye?"

Ah, in everything we have lost the secret. We
think not of others, but of ourselves.

"It is, of course," says Lord Frederic Hamilton,
"the easy fashion now to sneer at Victorian standards.
To my mind they embody all that is clean and sound in
the nation.   It does not follow that because Victorians
revelled in hideous wallpapers and loved ugly furniture,
that therefore their points-of-view were mistaken ones.

There are things more important than wallpapers. They certainly liked the obvious in painting, in music, and perhaps in literature, but it hardly seems to follow logically from that that their conceptions of a man's duty to his wife, family, and country were necessarily false ones.   They were not afflicted with the perpetual modern restlessness, nor did they spend 'their time in nothing else, but either to tell, or to hear, some new thing'; still, all their ideas seem to me eminently sweet and wholesome."

CHAPTER IX

EXAMPLES IN LOVE

It is the unconscious, rather than the conscious, which is the important factor in personality and intelligence. The unconscious furnishes the formative material out of which our judgments, our beliefs, our ideals, and our characters are shaped.—MORTON PRINCE.

Before marriage this question should be put: Will you continue to be satisfied with this woman's conversation until old age? Everything else in marriage is transitory.—NIETZSCHE.

WHEN we consider that a son born into a family of ancient lineage and of inspiring traditions, surrounded from infancy by objects of the greatest beauty, accustomed from childhood to the intimate friendship of the great, sent for his education to a school like Eton, and a university like Oxford, when we consider that a child so caressed by fortune and so nurtured by privilege does very often, as the first free act of his manhood, marry someone quite unsuitable to his place in the social hierarchy, such as a chorus girl out of a comic opera, we have reason to conclude that something was wanting in his circumstances, or his upbringing, which was essential to wisdom and happiness.

It is now a commonplace of political reform that education is a chief safeguard of the state. Our politicians tell us that when the democracy is well housed and thoroughly educated, all those economic problems which darken the future of civilisation will rise like mists and leave humanity in the full sunlight of millennium.

But democracy can never be better housed than Fashion, and never more carefully educated than the sons of Fashion. If, then, with all the blessings of beautiful houses and a system of education consecrated by centuries of piety, the sons of Fashion commit the greatest of follies at the outset of their career, and afterwards often live in a contemptible manner, spending their mature manhood, these sons of aristocracy, merely as spectators of the national life—the destinies of which are so largely in the hands of self-educated men from the lower ranks of society—how shall we look for salvation to the schoolmaster and the architect?

Something else, manifestly, is essential to safety.

It is scarcely an exaggeration to say that great numbers of young men in fashionable society pick up their wives just as a sensualist picks up a woman in the street. They are attracted by artifices which the prostitute has brought to perfection by long practice; they are knocked over by a calculated audacity, an unblushing but frequently an affected animalism, a licentiousness which is often as much put on as the

complexion or the eyebrows; they lose their heads
to the heel of a shoe and their hearts to the suffocation
of a scent—these young men who have been brought
up with every advantage of environment, education,
and tradition.

The chorus girl whom they find so seductive at a
table in a restaurant, so intoxicating in the padded re-
cesses of a motor-car, is a person of no education and of
few morals; she would not for the world walk the pave-
ments at night, but she would not scruple to sell herself
into a union, legal or illegal, with a rich man for whom
she entertains no deep affection. She belongs, as a rule,
to the lower middle classes, and has spent her childhood
in the suburbs. Her solitary cleverness is a faculty for
imitation; she can affect a drawl of boredom, has all
the phrases of smart society on the tip of her tongue,
and can powder her chin in public with the very gesture
of a duke's daughter. Fundamentally she is as ignorant as a Red Indian.

That a young Englishman of the highest class in
the land, with all the brilliant and beautiful women of
the world to choose from, should select such a trivial
little baggage as this for the mate of his soul and the
companion of his life, is not a matter for amusement or
amazement, but a fact of great social importance.

It brings us, I think, face to face with an evil which is
corrupting the whole body of civilisation like a cancer—
an arrest of moral growth, a refusal of vital tissues to

follow the law of their being, a stoppage in the development of the human soul.

Coleridge saw this danger long ago, and realised its infinite importance:

> All the evil achieved by Hobbes, and the whole School of Materialists, will appear inconsiderable if it be compared with the mischief effected and occasioned by the sentimental philosophy of Sterne, and his numerous imitators.
>
> The vilest appetites and the most remorseless inconstancy towards their objects, acquired the titles of the *Heart, the irresistible Feelings, the too tender Sensibility;* and if the frosts of prudence, the icy chains of human law, thawed and vanished at the genial warmth of Human *Nature,* who could help it?   It was an amiable weakness!
>
> About this time, too, the profanation of the word Love rose to its height.
>
> The French naturalists, Buffon and others, borrowed it from the sentimental novelists; the Swedish and English philosophers took the contagion; and the Muse of Science condescended to seek admission into the salons of Fashion and Frivolity, *rouged* like a harlot, and with the harlot's wanton leer.

He goes on to say, in words which after a hundred years are still applicable to the condition of human society:

> I know not how the annals of guilt could be better forced into the service of virtue than by such a comment on the present paragraph as would be afforded by a selection from the sentimental correspondence produced in courts of justice within the last thirty years, fairly

translated into the true meaning of the words and the natural object and purpose of the infamous writers.

The sentimental correspondence produced in the divorce court of our own days seems to me a document of the gravest sociological importance. No one can read the tragic or stupid effusions of respondents and co-respondents without an immense wonder at the ignorance of the human race, and a profound compassion for its victims. Those letters, if we read them with the sympathy they deserve, remembering, in spite of their construction and grammar, their crudeness and *naïveté*, their vulgarity and slang, that they are written by actual men and women, men and women anxious for happiness and capable of suffering, men and women, too, whose right-thinking is of importance to the rest of us, those letters, I think, witness to a colossal blunder on the part of society.

After all, the young man of Fashion and the powdered girl from the chorus are only children. They are at the door of experience, on the threshold of freedom, when they make their disastrous mistake. If the youth is persuaded that he can be permanently happy in the society of a girl no better educated, no sweeter-minded, no purer and holier in the true sense of these words, than the strumpets of Coventry Street; and if, on her part, the girl is convinced that the *summum bonum* is wealth, that possessions are the end of existence, that a title or a fortune solves all the difficulties of life; if this be so, then the fault is not in themselves that they are such moral and intellectual underlings, but in the state of society.

When I consider society's preparation for marriage, and its whole attitude towards love, I regard the divorce court not only as an inevitable institution of civilisation, but as one of the most merciful of our humanitarian and philanthropic organisations—indeed the kindest of all rescue societies. Like Coleridge, I regard marriage by the Registrar as "*reverential* to Christianity"; for it seems to me the very height of blasphemy that people who marry without the noblest conception of love in their souls should approach the altar of God and there make vows which only the sweetest purity can consecrate and only the most religious virtue can hope to keep. Far better that the fashionable marriage of our times should have no more religious pretensions than the hiring of a piano or the engaging of a bedroom, and that as soon as the unhappy couple have come to their senses, and realise that to live together in daily communion of mind and soul is an intolerable torture, they should be set free to make, if not a wiser choice, at least another shot.

No society with such a spirit as ours has the smallest right to condemn divorce. Its children not only have an absolute title to divorce, but just cause to bring against society, out of their own miseries, an indictment charging it with the crimes of the pimp and the pander.

Divorce can be regarded only as reprehensible in a society which makes the elevation of love a chief object of education, and itself sets the noblest examples in this highest of all human relationships. The children of devoted parents, parents who sacrificed everything to the highest spiritual interests of their children, are alone without excuse in that court of mercy.

No one will claim that Fashion labours in this direction; but how many perceive that the whole tendency of Fashion in this matter is towards the *degradation* of love? Almost every influence it possesses, so far as I am able to judge, is brought to bear on love with the sole purpose of degrading what the sentimentalist only profaned.

I am not speaking of a direct didactic addressed by society to the consciousness of mankind. I am speaking of Atmosphere—that power which penetrates to the huge workshop of the mind which we now call the unconscious. The atmosphere of our day, lacking the vigour of a moral purpose, has the exhausting and atrophying closeness of a hothouse. It is created by loose thinking. It fills the air with multiplying fallacies. It preys upon the unconscious mind with a thousand suggestions, making for self-indulgence. It undoes without effort all the painful work of the schoolmaster. It wipes the slate clean of religion. It is an atmosphere inimical to moral health and absolutely destructive of spiritual aspiration.

We must be honest with ourselves and confront the truth of our times. The profanation of love by the sentimentalist has ceased. The language of Sterne, which moved Coleridge to indignation, moves Fashion only to laughter; all that antique talk of *sensibility* is held in derision, as out of date now as the fainting heroines of Thackeray and Dickens. Society to-day is more honest, more brutal. It has ceased to make any pretence to idealism. Adultery has discarded the romantic cloak of Romeo, and comes laughing to the assignation in the modernised undress of Don Juan. The whole atmosphere is changed. It is more honest. It is more loyal to the lower nature. Love is a joke, one of the amusements, one of the adventures, one of the sports, one of the recreations of society. To take it seriously is both provincial and dangerous. It must be treated as our fathers treated flirtation. The business of life is money; one of its recreations, like bridge or golf, is the sexual instinct. The romantic woman learns at her first fence that she must choose between hysterics and "lovers."

This atmosphere, which is now almost universal throughout society, I regard as fatal to the higher life of the human race. It makes passion one of the indecencies of life—a subject for grins and whispers, a theme for *revue*, an opportunity for gossip, a matter on all fours with a dirty story. It is a destructive

COLONEL CHARLES REPINGTON

atmosphere.   It kills love as readily as an abortionist
kills a future human being.

Perhaps the reader will pardon me if I venture to
suggest to Fashion a moment's consideration of the
pedigree of love.   I should not dream of making this
suggestion in an essay of the present character were
I not convinced that even among educated people
slovenliness of thought may lead to calamitous consequences; as witness in the last fifty years the philosophical havoc wrought among educated people by so
foolish a phrase as *the struggle for existence*, few men
perceiving that a creature in existence cannot possibly
struggle for what it already possesses, and that the
real struggle in nature — a key to the spiritual mystery — is a struggle for *improvement*, and that the
greatest force in that struggle is not egotism, selfishness, and brutal aggression, but a most significant
co-operation.

Let Fashion ask itself how it comes to exist.   Let
it look at the stage on which the human comedy is
enacted.   That stage has a history; all the players
have a pedigree; history and pedigree alike stretch
back into an utterly immeasurable past.   Life, whatever we choose to make it, can only be treated lightly or
derisively by a lunatic.   It is far too old a thing, too
wonderful an antiquity, to be treated like one of the
crazes of the last season.   It is worthy of interest,
worthy, perhaps, of reverence and gratitude.   Only in

10

the delusions of an idiot can it be divorced from its context of the eternal existence.

There was once no universe. The horizons of space stretched onwards into a distance which had neither boundary wall nor ultimate sheer precipice descending with a rush into the void of nothingness.

There was no time. Duration was a dial with neither figures nor hands.

There was no life. The conjugation of existence rested at the First Person of the Present Tense: I AM.

Out of this just comprehensible abidance of the Infinite within the Infinite came the birth of life.

There was movement. In this movement there was direction. The universe was born.

Of that stupendous creation three things may be affirmed at this day with some confidence: it is the work of Mind, it is altogether too huge for an idle fancy, and love, if not its sole object, is at least one of its preponderant forces.

So far as our planet is concerned we can imagine its history without many of the means which appear to have moulded its destinies, but it is beyond the reach of imagination to think of that eventful chronicle without the love which exists in the tigress for its cubs, the wren for its nestlings, and the mother for her children.

Love, then, is a great thing. Even as lust it is a great thing. For, steadily regarded, lust is seen as the manger used by evolution for the first cradle of self-sacrifice. Out of lust, blind animal lust, which is a clean thing, and not a prurient thing like a Kirchner picture, has come the highest love we know, the love which takes no thought for itself.

If you regard the common love of man and woman just as it is, remembering its history, and seeing what it can achieve, you will find that it is not to be placed where Fashion loves to place it, among the indecencies of civilisation. It is a tremendous thing in a tremendous universe, born of the first movement of Antecedent Existence, and bearing in its seed the highest purposes of the creative power; something to be exalted, reverenced, perfected; something that seems as though it had the power, as nothing else on earth, to make gods of us, when the end is reached; something which only a devil could profane, and in which only a fool could see nothing for marvel and thanksgiving.

Such is the love which brings a grin to painted lips and amusement to "clinkered souls."

Fashion, I hope, will observe that in this brief summary of evolution I have made no appeal to religion, and advanced no claim for love which is not justified by the findings of physical science. I am anxious to persuade people on the grounds of reason alone that love is a respectable thing. It has a pedigree whose origin is lost to us only in the origin of the Absolute. It has a history which is as sublime as the history of the visible universe. And at every point in that mysterious struggle for perfection which we call evolution it is found working for the destiny towards which all creation is moving, and of which no man has been able to imagine the end.

To degrade love, then, to make it something base or trivial, is to interfere with the first mechanism of evolution. And to do this is as much to endanger the safety of the human race as squirting corrosive acid into the eye would endanger sight. Fashion, when it plays with love, is indeed playing with a fire that may consume the house of life. For love is essential to existence; and the evolution of love is essential to higher existence. If we use this tremendous power loosely we hinder its purpose; if we use it vilely we bring creation to a standstill. For we transitory creatures in an endless chain of existence, receiving from the past and giving to the future, we are the reeds through which this power would blow the hymn of creation, the laudamus of the universe, the lyric of the human heart; and if we behave as if for us and for us alone—for our vulgarities, vanities, indecencies, and egoisms—everything that exists has been created, we silence the music of God, and in ourselves at least bring the divine purpose to a standstill.

Domestic unhappiness is a consequence of wrong thinking in society. Wrong-thinking is fatal to right-living. The atmosphere is charged with illusion, and illusion is the fertile parent of disaster. However beautifully a child may be surrounded in his nonage, and however carefully he may be educated in his youth, he comes at manhood into a world which is apparently organised solely for the many purposes of self-indulgence, and which is certainly not organised for any far-off divine event, a world whose whole thesis of life is vitiated by a false premise.

In this world, blinded by its artificial brilliance and bewildered by its rush towards excitement and sensation, in this world, where there is no shrine for worship and no altar for silence and reflection, in this cynical and disillusioned world, where to be serious is to be deserted as a bore, and to be virtuous is to be ridiculed as a prig, the youth makes his choice of a wife, and the girl makes her choice of a husband.

They are brought together by festivity. Their personalities touch in a racket. Their first embrace, to the music of a negro band, is made in a dance from the jungle. Nothing in the atmosphere suggests seriousness. No one utters a warning, no one breathes a caution. On the contrary, to think is to find oneself stranded. Flung into the rush and deafened by the noise, the one thing to do is to keep one's feet; to keep one's head—that is impossible, and useless.

Everything declares that life is a masquerade, and self-indulgence the sole purpose of creation. The daughter learns from her mother, the son from his father. Everyone is selfish. There is only one reasonable pursuit—a good time. And this is the good time;

this life of pleasure, this life of eating and drinking, of dancing and flirting, of crowds and crushes, of adventures in sex, of licence and cynicism, of excitement and selfishness, of money and ostentation. "Is he rich? Then, my dear, why hesitate? Marry him at once."

It is in such an atmosphere as this that the marriages of Fashion are made. Youth enters by the gate of comedy and goes out through the door of tragedy. The embrace of the jazz is dissolved by the decree absolute of the divorce court.

This is the example set by Fashion in a matter which is foundational to the safety and happiness of the State.

Civilisations, let us assure ourselves, are far more vulnerable on their domestic side than on their economic side. The home is the unit of the nation. Family life is its great assurance. If a state would not perish it must see that its homes are the altars of human happiness, must realise that its economic activity has for its main object the human happiness of the family. A bad example in this matter is a thousand times more perilous than any propaganda of Bolshevism. No gospel of anarchy, indeed, could exist for nine days in a state founded on the sure satisfaction of family life. It is only by the door of domestic unhappiness that political unrest enters a community.

There was a time, as Sainte-Beuve says, when the follies and sins of Fashion were prevented, by the exclusiveness of society itself, from penetrating to the

bourgeoisie and the proletariat.   But since the day of
Sainte-Beuve few things done by Fashion lack the service of a publicity agent.   Indeed, Fashion itself tells
the story; Fashion itself gives its photograph to the
world.   There is no shame.   There is no desire even for
the humility of anonymity.   Fashion, flattered and
amused by the invitation of the other classes, is now
as ready to bare its bosom to the lending library as to
give a testimonial to a wig-maker or maker of com-
plexions.   The cry of the very lowest stratum is now
the cry for "a good time."

The blunder of Fashion is caused by forgetfulness.
It has forgotten the past of humanity, and it forgets
that humanity has a future.   It occupies its place in
time without gratitude and without any feeling of
responsibility.   The past is a blank, the future a void.
The long ancestry of mankind is no more to it than a back
number of *Punch;* the future destinies of the human
race no more to it than the weather of the next century.

It is just for want of this sense of proportion that
Fashion has lost the capacity for seriousness.   It sees
the cosmos in a ballroom, and the human race in its own
mirror.   It is an inch thinking of itself as the whole
mile, a wave thinking of itself as all the ocean, a syllable
in Hamlet thinking of itself as the soul of Shakespeare.

It sees creation so completely out of perspective,
and so totally ignores the whole chronicle of history,
that it has even lost the sense of a local patriotism.

It does not feel itself in any way responsible for the welfare of England. And so it comes about that Fashion recklessly sets examples which are fatal to the stability of England's national greatness, examples which menace the very foundations of English character, examples of which the worst of all is this example in the field of love —an example which corrupts human life at its very source and reduces the great security of national existence to a problem for discussion among novelists.

When a school of philosophers tells me that many mysteries in psychology may be traced back to "sex repressions," I wonder if it has never occurred to this school that what it regards as a "repression" may in truth be an "obsession," and that this sediment of sex which it professes to find in so many minds is not the consequences of evolution, but the result of mass *suggestion*—symptomatic of an immoral age, but not characteristic of mankind in its health and sanity.

Where love is lacking, "sex" lurks. Love is a cleansing power; "sex" is nothing more than lust in a state of decomposition.

Does it not demand a diseased mind to admit the contention of Remy de Gourmont that the statuary of Greece is immortal because it is sexual, and sexual because it is nude? Is not the "sex" in the mind of de Gourmont, and not in the statuary? There are minds which are like a printer's error: they can only see immorality in immortality.

CHAPTER X

WOMANHOOD

The mother of debauchery is not joy, but joylessness.—
NIETZSCHE.

*My mother's character was a blend of extreme simplicity
and great dignity, with a limitless gift of sympathy for others.
I can say with perfect truth that, throughout her life, she suc-
ceeded in winning the deep love of all those who were brought
into constant contact with her.—*LORD FREDERIC HAMILTON.

ONE markedly new thing in English life has accompanied the decline in morals and manners. This new
thing is a new spirit in women.

The Times recently reported Mr. Justice Horridge's
summing up to a jury in these words:

> You have to try to consider the matter of the co-re-
> spondent's conduct from the point of view of society as it
> has existed since the War. You and I may think that the
> good old times, when married women did not knock about
> with men quite so much as they do, and girls did not go
> unchaperoned into ballrooms, were the right times. We
> may think it would be good if those times came back
> again, but you have to consider this case from the point of
> view of what is going on all around us.

In these words the judge gave to the *dramatis personæ* of our age a new character: *The woman who knocks about.* The expression is a useful one.   It points to an absence of all direction.   The woman who knocks about is not walking to the devil with her eyes open.   She is not courting disaster with a guide book to show her the way.   She is not looking for trouble with a microscope.   Her peril is absence of motive.   She does not know why she is living.   She is not at a loose end; existence itself is a loose end.   She knocks about, like a cork in the sea.

The Woman Who Knocks About has superseded the Particular Woman.

All round London there is a vast and spreading circle of villadom.   A few years ago these suburbs were the strongholds of family life.   Here lived people who mocked the extravagances of fashionable society, and were blissfully unaware of its deeper iniquities.   The husbands went by train to the City; the house-proud wives remained at home with the children.   The life of each little community centred in the home, and had its circumference in the parish, of which they were proud and in which they worked.   You found benevolence there, a sense of neighbourly responsibility, a desire for mental improvement, above all things, self-sacrifice for the sake of the children.

To-day, many of these women go to London almost as regularly as their husbands go to the City.   They are spoken of as "Season Ticket Women."   Their excuse

is the shop—their attraction is the restaurant. They
have contracted a passion for crowds, for adventures,
for excitement. They knock about with other people
who are knocking about. In a garish restaurant, with
an orchestra playing dance music, and crowds of people
waiting for tables, they light their cigarettes, drink
their liqueurs, and feel that they are at the very centre
of fashionable life.

Not many of these women are faithless to their marriage vows. But they are faithless to their children,
faithless to their homes, faithless to the Church, faithless to the great moral traditions of their country. A
few of them take the next step. They conceive a
passion—perhaps for some boy in the Air Service.
They pay for his meals, buy him neckties and cigarettes,
take him to the music-hall. He seems to them much
more heroic than their hard-working husbands. They
come to regard duty as dull, and the narrow way as a
rut. A delightful feeling of romance blinds them to the
nobler qualities, the enduring virtues, the firmer manhood of their husbands. Any young blackguard in a
uniform has for these middle-aged imbeciles the linea-
ments of Romeo and the character of Hector. Self-
respect is consumed in the transient flame of a romantic
excitement; they go to the devil.

Fashion is fond of laughing at the pretensions of
the middle class. But those pretensions are merely its
own spirit on a smaller income.

I have visited many hostels occupied by girls of education, who are training for professional careers. The casualties in this quarter are the casualties of semi-starvation. These girls, many of them fresh and grace-ful, some of them most beautiful, are hectic, excitable, unstable, neurotic. When they are hungry they drink tea, when they are racked by nerves they smoke cigar-ettes. A slight illness brings them to collapse. Many die when they are quite young.

Who is to blame?

These girls, fighting for their careers, spend every penny they can scrape together on raiment. They stand no chance if they are not fashionably dressed. Artificial silk means more to them than honest wool. The good Englishman in India, denying himself a holi-day at home, sending all the money he can save to his daughter in England, believing that his self-sacrifice is providing for her health and happiness, learns by one mail that she has caught a cold and by the next that she is dead.

There is a more sordid aspect of this corruption. The vice of our public streets has undergone a remark-able change. There is a new race of immoral women. They come from offices and shops. They are young, and the glamour of the summit has bewitched them. They desire the life of fashion, the life of indelicate clothes, gilded restaurants, the theatre, and the night-club.

They are not vicious. They have none of the criminal

instincts of those women who complain of their competi-
tion. Ask them what they want, and they will tell you
"a good time." That is all. They want to see life.
They have looked up to our highest, and in their own
small way would copy them. So they sell first their
modesty and then their virtue. It is the price they pay
for "a good time."

We sell our honours for money by the hand of our
Prime Minister and in the name of our Sovereign.
These girls give their honour for the same exchange.
Money can buy anything, even what is called an
"illegal operation."

Go lower still. There is a collapse of the most primitive virtue among girls who live in the slums of our
seaport towns. They are so shameless that they get
themselves rowed out to incoming ships that they may
make sure of a sailor when the vessel comes into port, be
he Lascar, Negro, or Chinaman. Parliament has just
lately had to move in this matter, so great, so open, is
the scandal; it is now enacted that no woman may enter
a port "for the purpose of prostitution," or be rowed out
to a ship for that same object. [1]

[1] (1) A prostitute shall not enter or be on board any ship or vessel in
any port, dock, or harbour for the purpose of prostitution, and a person
shall not take any prostitute on board any ship for any such purpose.

(2) It shall be the duty of every port, dock, and harbour authority
by the exercise of any powers possessed by them in that behalf, to take
all reasonable steps to prevent persons from resorting to any port,
dock, or harbour, of which they are the authority, or any ship or vessel
therein, for purposes of prostitution.

Some of these girls are the very dregs of degradation. Most of them, however, are inspired by the same motive which moves the millionaire to activity. They want money. And they want money for the same reason that the millionaire's wife and daughter want it; for display, for rich food, for excitement, for "a good time." Tell them that it is wrong to be immodest, wicked to be immoral, and they will point to the heights, laughing you to scorn for a canting, psalm-singing charlatan. They have ceased to feel the smallest respect for virtue. After all, to the eyes of eternal Judgment, is there much difference in moral values between the summit and the abyss?

There comes from social workers in all quarters of our congested and violent life a cry that borders on despair. The womanhood of the nation is becoming corrupt. There is a decided movement among the older women towards drunkenness, among the younger women towards vice. A lady who has visited the common lodging-houses of London says that educated girls of a quite decent class are now to be found there among the vilest women. Out of twenty-eight inmates in one case alone fifteen were found with venereal disease.

Even where the Commandments are not broken the spirit of virtue is ignored. The demand of these women is for excitement. They cannot rest. To be patient is to be tortured. To be at home is to be imprisoned. They clamour to live like the Rich. The old ideal of the English mother, finding her heaven in her home and her immortality in her children, is no longer the fashion. The music of life has become livelier, and they would dance. This passion for knocking about has descended to lower levels. I open my newspaper this morning and find the following report of "A Girl's Gay Life":

> Describing herself as the private secretary of a financial magnate, N. T., the pretty daughter of a Treforest (Glamorgan) collier, made her home at the Westgate Hotel, Newport (Mon.), from December 22nd to January 1st. There she is alleged to have spent much time in the lounge, smoking cigarettes and entertaining young men to champagne suppers. She left without paying her account.
>
> When charged at Newport yesterday with false pretences involving nearly £12, with 6s. for cigarettes, the Bench were informed that the girl, who was supposed by her mother to be employed at an office at Cardiff, had for two years been leading a gay life, supported by moneys from a source which she would not divulge.
>
> The girl's father offered to pay the debt, and as the prosecution did not press the matter the Bench bound her over for six months.

There is here only one element which makes the case notable, and so brings it into the limelight of public attention; *the girl could not pay her bill*. Anyone who knows the chief cities of the provinces is familiar with the same spirit in thousands of girls. It is universal. Let the traveller go into the "lounge of the great hotels in Birmingham, Manchester, Liverpool, Leeds, Edinburgh, Glasgow, and he will find those places occupied mainly by girls of the town, extravagantly dressed, rouged, painted, powdered, either accompanied by men or keeping their eyes open for a likely stranger entering from behind the screens.   They are out "on the loose." The labourer's daughter is as determined as the daughter of the clerk and shop assistant to have "a good time."

Descend to an even lower level.   To realise the condition of modern childhood in our great cities, let your mind ponder the necessity for enactments concerning children under sixteen years of age and children *under fourteen years of age.*   Where are the mothers of these children?   And what have been the conditions of their home life?   Is it unreasonable to ask questions of the womanhood of the country?   Is it not folly to wander away into the side-issue of economic conditions?

The novelist, Miss Clemence Dane, has lately taken up the question of cruelty to children, the awful and unspeakable cruelty which exists in all our great cities and towns, and which, for some unknown reason, is punished so lightly by the magistrates.

She writes of "that vilest of all cruelties, child assault."   I quote the following instances from her article:

How these men, guilty of unspeakable offences against children, are too often dealt with in practice, the following random extracts from newspapers may show. *I omit the unprintable details.*

For attempted assault on a child of four. Bound over on account of previous good character.

For assault on child of seven. Sentence: six months.

For stealing leather from employers (same case): six months.

For assault on baby of four. Sentence: £2 fine.

For assaulting and infecting a child of seven. Sentence: twelve months.

For assaulting and infecting a child of seven: bound over.

For assaulting (on the same day) two little girls: bound over.

For assault on three small children—evidence unfit for publication. Sentence: £5 fine.

For assault on child of twelve (six previous convictions for the same offence). Sentence: three months.

All this horror exists beneath the smiling surface of our national life. We may avert our heads, but it is there. We may refuse to think about it, but it is destroying us. Yes, destroying us; for all this horror and all this moral lassitude and all this joyless turning to debauchery for relief from the tedium of modern life, all this means that the great central ideal of the human race, a pure womanhood, is ceasing to inspire the heart of mankind.

Ask social workers how it is that the children of our cities are so rapidly depraved, and they will tell you that the mothers are careless, that the mothers are often themselves utterly depraved, and that, in any case, the idea of parental authority is passing away.

11

In almost every case, indeed I find it hard to discover a single exception, the mothers of girls who go to the dogs in their teens are women without moral energy and without ideals.

We are not reading of Siberia, where girls of thirteen are often mothers, and where children of ten are often used as prostitutes; we are reading of the greatest country of the world, and of the greatest cities in that country.   Is it not folly to wander away into the side-issue of economic conditions?   Women are becoming bad.   There is a moral declension.   It has nothing to do with economics.   It is a spirit appearing in the Richest and the Poorest.   Housing and education are no valid factors in this problem.   In every circle of the community, and in all conditions, morality has lost its grip.   The particular woman is everywhere an anachronism.

As I write there is a photograph on my mantelpiece of Eucken.   I never turned its face to the wall during the War.   Often I looked at his message on the photograph.   "Rudolf Eucken sendet besten Gruss," followed by an invitation to Jena.

I take one of his books from my shelves.   This is what I read:

At the present time, when the State is engrossed by economic and other constantly changing problems of the day, we need a community which attaches importance to the inner problems of humanity, and which directs our life towards eternal aims and values.

Good!

If morality be weakened, then life is robbed of a strong impulse, of an ennobling power, and of a dominant aim. . . . The salt of life is then lacking, which alone can keep it fresh and healthy.

Thus spoke Rudolf Eucken in 1913.
What did Alfred Zimmern say of this great moralist in 1914?

. . . men like Harnack, Eucken, and Wilamowitz, who would repudiate all intellectual kinship with Machiavelli and Nietzsche—men who are leaders of European thought . . . publicly support and encourage the policy and standpoint of a Government which, according to British ideas, has acted with criminal wickedness and folly, and so totally misunderstands the conduct and attitude of Great Britain as honestly to regard us as hypocritically treacherous to the highest interests of civilisation.

Zimmern realised the peril of the position. It was not the criminal statesman or militarist in Germany who raised our greatest problem, but the chief moralists, the most noble and persuasive philosophers, of modern Germany. Eucken regarded our fealty to Belgium as an act of hypocrisy!

What are we to say, then? Eucken on the side of Prussianism! Eucken supporting the odious and pagan theory that the State has nothing to do with ethics! If this madness is possible in one of the noblest men of our time, what are we to expect from our frivolous women, our women of villadom, our girls of the back-street and the slum?

Are we to throw up our hands, like the Russians, and say that man cannot war against the spirit of his time, and that the Atlantic of tendency will always defeat the mop of moral idealism?

Are we going from bad to worse? Is the present time only the prelude to a millennium of anarchy? Are we living in another Drift Age—the whole mass of humanity shifting like a glacier towards destruction? Morality—is it only an opinion, a convenience, a superstition? We who believe in self-control, in self-sacrifice, in self-improvement; are we, perhaps, very old-fashioned people whose days should have been cast in the times of the Puritans?

It is not in English nature, I firmly believe, I earnestly hope, ever to despair of a great cause. There is something in an Englishman, as Goethe knew and acknowledged, which is superior to the greater intelligence of German professors; it is our English character, our strong common sense, our instinct for right. Eucken's defection must not, nay, *cannot*, destroy the very centre of our patriotism—faith in human perfection. The times may be opposed to us; but opposed to the times is something stronger than the clock, stronger than evil—the purpose of the universe. We know, too, that the very nature of evil is to defeat itself. After a little the palate craves for wholesome bread, and finally the digestion refuses poison. There may be a period before us of great moral darkness, but the sun will return and we shall see again the one straight narrow path that leads forward.

In the meantime, are we merely to wait till the fever has burnt itself out, and the patient cries in the name of God for "something bitter"?

Perhaps those who care for the moral foundations of the State might be content to stand aside and wait for the fever to burn itself out, if the fever had its rise in some folly of the flesh. But who that greatly cares for his country can bear to wait for the end of *this* fever, which has its rise in the moral nature of the individual, which altogether disowns responsibility, which rejects the higher life of the human spirit, which is against all seriousness, all aspiration, all reverence, all modesty, and the most dreadful symptom of which is its corruption of Womanhood?

"There can be no time," said Lord Jeffrey, in a notable censure, "in which the purity of female character can fail to be of the first importance to every community. . . . The character and morality of women exercises already a mighty influence upon the happiness and respectability of the nation. But if they should ever cease to be pure . . . to overawe profligacy, and to win and to shame men into decency, fidelity, and love of unsullied virtue . . . domestic happiness and private honour will be extinguished, and public spirit and national industry most probably annihilated along with them."

Those words were written more than a hundred years ago; their occasion was not the corruption of women who knock about; they were inspired by the trivial poetry of Thomas Moore! What had Lord Jeffrey said of these days? The crumbling has become a land-slide.

Where the corruption of womanhood is concerned, no one who hopes for a greater race can stand idle, good women least of all.

But what are we to do?

I answer: If the nation is going wrong, it is being led wrong. Who are the leaders? The most powerful of all our leaders, I reply, is Fashion—not Parliament, not Church, not Press—but Fashion. If, then, we would go in a right direction instead of a wrong direction, those who set the nation its most conspicuous examples must be, not equivocally, not half-heartedly, not wearily, but enthusiastically on the side of Excellence.

CHAPTER XI

CONCLUSION

Society originates in the need of a livelihood, but it exists for the sake of life.—ARISTOTLE.

> *The open secret flashes on the brain,*
> *As if one almost guessed it, almost knew*
> *Whence we have sailed and voyage whereunto.*
> FREDERIC MYERS.

Never forget: The higher we soar, the smaller do we appear to those who cannot fly.—NIETZSCHE.

IN the course of this essay I have advanced certain propositions which may be summarised as follows:

Fashion, because of its conspicuous position in the State, exercises the greatest of all influences on the nation.

The influences of modern Fashion are injurious to the peaceful evolution of the British Commonwealth, being the influences of ostentation, self-indulgence, lawlessness, cynicism, and frivolity.

The influence of Iniquity is not to be so greatly feared by a nation as the influence of Folly.

It is by the domestic door, rather than the economic, that violence enters a State.

The social, political, and moral health of a community

depends mainly upon its attitude towards life, that is to say, its theory of existence.

In a rational theory of existence it is impossible to divorce time from its context of eternity, place from its context of infinity, man from his context of evolution.

At the head of a nation there should be an aristocracy of intelligence whose manner of life exhibits the truth of this theory.

Out of these propositions, reminding myself of all the goodness and sweetness that exist in England, I develop the concluding proposition, forced upon me by the state of public morality, *that goodness is not enough.*

This idea is not new. Aristotle made a vital distinction between the excellence of conduct and the higher excellence of intelligence. But Aristotle did not develop his thesis to its revolutionary conclusion. That work was accomplished some four centuries later in the hills of Galilee, accomplished, but afterwards, except for a few, hidden away out of the knowledge of man for nearly two thousand years. We have forgotten that morality is not enough, altogether forgotten that Christ proclaimed His theory of existence as good news for mankind, Himself as the light of the world.

When it is perceived that goodness is not enough, a revolution takes place in the human mind. It flashes upon us that it is an altogether different thing from merely being good to love excellence. No longer do we think of death as an end or the "Last Day" as an examination. We understand how it is that some perfectly good people do not inspire our affections or are even positively tiresome. We see how it is that life is so provincial and dull. Goodness is not enough. There is something beyond morality. Love of God; how different from obedience to the Mosaic Law! We feel ourselves flying, through the eternity which now visibly surrounds us on every side, as birds fly in a summer sky. Joy takes a new meaning. Power clamours for a new definition. We are not in a rut; we are not shut down in a pit. We are children of God, and, if children, then heirs of eternal life; and eternal life is evolution, evolution towards ever greater power, ever greater understanding, ever greater bliss, "the reason always attentive, but always satisfied." This, I think, is the natural consequence of discovering our context in eternity. We enter on a new birth, a birth of joy and thanksgiving.

I am coming to believe that we may now be moving towards another and a far greater renaissance than that which ended the long drowse of the middle ages. I feel that this present darkness has become so stifling, and this present confusion so inextricable, that we may expect humanity to rescue itself from a reversion to barbarism by one of those great forward movements which at long intervals in history have saved evolution from a fatal halt or a destructive recession.

What will this next step be? A step, I think, from the excellence of conduct to the excellence of intelli-

gence; a step from a pious hope into a definite intellectual conception.   The present depression of humanity
has its origin, I believe, solely in man's degraded sense
of his origin.   The human race feels itself like a rat in a
trap.   We began in the mud and shall end in the mud.
Life is reaching the end of its tether.   There is nothing
more to discover.   The only business in the world is to
get what you want before somebody else gets hold of it.
Humanity rots for a new definition of life.

I feel that distracted man would now welcome one
who made plain to him that the gate of existence still
stands wide open, that human life is no cul-de-sac but a
thoroughfare, and that across the grey ocean of morality there lies an undiscovered New World of spiritual
adventure.   To one who could convince humanity of its
context, could reveal to it the universe as a book from
which the page of earth *cannot* be torn, one who could
make it perceive that evolution is at work now in the
spirit of man, just as it was at work millions of years
ago on the separate elements of protoplasm, to such a
one I believe the human race would listen, at first with
incredulity, but afterwards with relief and gladness.
Then, if so, the earth would find a new stirring of life,
such as it felt in the sixteenth century, when a dawn
broke on human history which was like the gates of
Paradise.

The renaissance of the sixteenth century was a turning back on the part of depressed humanity to the light

of Athenian culture. In that light men came to see a new world at their feet, and to speculate on a new universe around and within them.

Let me remind the reader, in the words of Professor Muirhead, what the most modern of the Greeks believed about man and his destiny. To Aristotle, "the nature of man is not that out of which he has developed, but that into which he is developing; not what he is at the lowest, but what he is at the highest; not what he is *born as* (to borrow a happy distinction), but what he is *born for*."

> A flower is not less a flower because of the earth out of which it springs, or a statue a statue because it is resolvable into carbonate of lime.
> The glory of the flower and of the statue is that their materials have been transfigured in the making of them, as it is the glory of their materials to be so transfigured.
> Similarly, it is the glory of the soul to have moulded and transfigured the body, just as it is the glory of the body to have been moulded and transfigured by the soul.[1]

Men of the middle ages, turning from superstition to walk in this enchanted garden of rational and fearless inquiry, brought to the earth a new dawn, and to the human race a new birth. They looked about them and felt themselves free. They stood upright on their feet, conscious of a new dignity in man. They were no longer slaves to the past; they were voyagers to the

[1] *Chapters from Aristotle's Ethics*, by J. H. Muirhead.

unimaginable future. As regards our own nation, over whose island cliffs that great dawn rose last of all the countries in Western Europe, the new birth was mainly the work of a small and virtuous aristocracy which had exhausted the monotony of superstition and was aware in itself of powers pressing for exercise. It was a spiritual palingenesis, as well as an intellectual awakening.

Erasmus, let us remind ourselves, extolled the English nobility to all mankind for its learning and its serious purpose. He compared its refined discourse at table with the profligate talk then fashionable amongst priests on the continent. The children of aristocracy were educated with a view to making them true leaders of the nation. Roger Ascham, that characteristic Englishman, attacked with matchless power every foreign influence which tended to deflect nobility from its gracious duty. Sir Thomas Elyot held that just as the angels nearest to the Throne of God were those most capable of adoration, so the aristocracy of a nation, grouped round its King, should be most capable of setting an example in all virtue to the other classes; by "the beams of their excellent wit" they were to direct "others of inferior understanding" into the way of "commodious living." Ascham could say in 1550, "Never has the English nobility been so learned."

Nor was this learning merely an ornament; a nobler spirit than humanism moved upon the face of those waters. Sir Thomas More, described by Erasmus as "the man of every hour," set the Commonwealth an ideal which to this day is far in advance of any democratic state. He saw that society existed for life, not for bread-earning. He hated the idea of overwork for mere wages, and claimed that the worker had a right to leisure for the cultivation of his mind. He opposed himself to the sporting landlord who, by turning his tillage to permanent pasture, robbed the State of its strongest citizens. He hated the cruelty of blood sports, opposed himself to capital punishment, and was a prison reformer of the most humane and sensible character. Private property had no religious nimbus for More; his passion for the Commonwealth led him so far that he desired even the abolition of capital. Man, the creature most dear to God, was the supreme object of his moral and intellectual affections, and to ennoble man to fill his mind with wonder and rejoicing, to lead him away from all that depressed his soul, to guide him onward and upward into those paths of the spirit which alone lead to his destiny, this was the desire of that noble intellect, that gentle heart, that characteristic good Englishman.

It was because the Renaissance proved in the end false to the aspiration of its highest minds that it lost power and flickered out into the gloom and twilight of disillusion. It looked back to the past, but not far enough, *and forgot to look forward.* It was unconscious of the eternity surrounding man, of which he is the inhabitant, and through which he is a voyager. It became, because of this short-sightedness, little more than a revival of paganism. Its fortunes fell into the hands of the Italianate Englishman, the mere intellectual fop. At the Restoration it was the possession of the coxcomb and the pedant, a thing without soul, a thing so shrunken and attenuated that it had no room for the spirit of humanity. Science saved it eventually from disrepute, and by the hand of Science its flag has been at least lifted from the gutter, and carried forward through the darkness of many troubled hours; but the glory and joy of it have departed. Men no longer feel that life is a blessing.

As one thinks of the fate of the Renaissance, one recalls a great saying by Coleridge: "Across the night of Paganism, Philosophy flitted on, like the lantern-fly of the tropics, a light to itself, and an ornament, but alas! no more than an ornament of the surrounding darkness." He showed how Christianity had revolutionised human thought. Philosophy sought to elevate the moral character by improving the intellect; Christianity *reversed the order*.

By relieving the mind from the distractions and importunities of the unruly passions, she improves the *quality* of the Understanding; while at the same time *she presents for its contemplation objects so great and so bright as cannot but enlarge the organ by which they are contemplated.*

No man taught more forcibly than Coleridge the necessity for preventing "the rank vapours that steam up from the corrupt heart," but no man saw more vividly that the cleansed heart is only a means to the infinitely greater end of an exalted spirit. "While morality," says Marsh, "is something more than prudence, religion—the spiritual life—is something more than morality." It is by realising his kinship with the universe that man becomes the creative agent of joy.

This, perhaps, is our way to a greater renaissance than that which illuminated the sixteenth century, and went astray in the seventeenth. He who would save the human race from darkness must go back to the light of the world, not to assert the claims of theology, not to strengthen the hands of clericalism, but simply to make faith in a spiritual purpose the very breath of human existence. Immortality must be an intellectual conviction, not an emotional uncertainty. Intelligence must become a passion.

Man is a creature most dear to God. He is a citizen of a universe that is infinite. He is the child of a duration that is eternal. He cannot be dislodged from infinity and eternity any more than a day can be dislodged from a year. Loyalty to his moral nature is necessary to the understanding of his destiny, but his true happiness lies in the exercise of his spiritual faculties. Until he comprehends the greatness of his glory,

and the unimaginable splendours of his inheritance, he
must be a creature of unrest and ever greater confusion.

> Now, in this is the excellency of Man, that he is made
> capable of a communion with his Maker, and, because
> capable of it, is unsatisfied without it; the soul being cut
> out (so to speak) to that largeness cannot be filled with
> less.

In this renaissance of the human spirit, which appears
to me our one way out from the present darkness, what
part, if it comes, will be played by England? What
part will be taken by the aristocracy, that is to say, by
the people at the head of the nation? Can Fashion
help us, can Mammon help us, to enter into a new
birth of the human spirit?

I think the work of preparation must be done by
others. I feel that our salvation will come from the
good of all classes—from the good among the aristocracy,
the good among the numerous middle classes, the good
among the manual workers—and that this work of
salvation will proceed from the knowledge that, beyond
obedience to morals, there is a boundless region of spiritual excellence waiting for the exploration of mankind.
The good will become our aristocracy when they
understand that goodness is not enough.

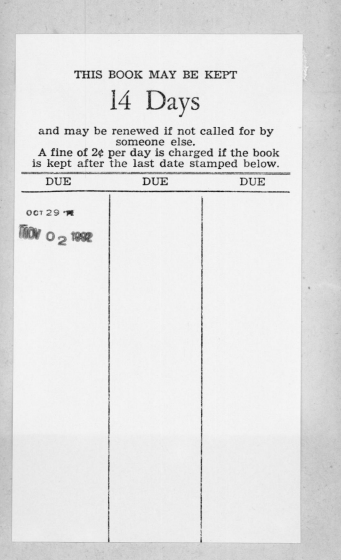